The **WISDOM** of a Fool

Who am I, other than who I am?
For how you perceive me to be, is who I am to you.
But that you may truly know me,
I have doff my name
and offered you all of me.

PRESS

The Day of the LORD

"Surely the day is coming; it will burn like a furnace.
All the arrogant and every evildoer will be stubble,
and that day that is coming will set them
on fire," says the LORD Almighty...

See, I will send you the prophet Elijah
before that great and dreadful day of the LORD comes.
He will turn the hearts of the fathers to their children,
and the hearts of the children to their fathers; or else
I will come and strike the land with a curse."
(Malachi 4:1-6)

Presented to

_____

From

_____

Date

_____

Message

_____

"He who speaks on his own
does so to gain honor for himself,
but he who works for the honor of the one who sent him
is a man of truth; there is nothing false about him."
(John 7:18)

6

I speak not in words taught by human wisdom
but in words taught by the Spirit.

"How much better to get wisdom than gold,
to choose understanding rather than silver!"
(Proverbs 16:16)

CONTENTS:

Traditionally the Table of Contents
provides a division of *chapters or articles*
in reference to the page for which it starts but
this Book is nothing like that. It is simply a
compilation of **My Thoughts on Paper.**
This book
covers a wide range of topics such as God,
Life, Truth, Love, Suffering, Forgiveness,
Education, Children, Parenting, Evil,
Religion, Wisdom, Peace, Greed
Sin, Money, War, Atheism,
Beauty, Politics, Death,
Deception, and more.
It also resolves to answer questions such as:

"Why does God allow so much pain and suffering?"

-

If everything was created by God,
then *Who* created God?

-

Are "True Things" Truth?

-

What does it mean to JUDGE NOT?

-

What are the key differences between
Catholic and Protestant Christianity?

-

The most "Ignorant" question ever asked.
And several other questions.

The latter part of this Book
gives a brief overview of various religions
(portrayed in alphabetical order).

PREFACE

I understand that there are many different types of people, each with their own unique questions and despite the fact that a vast majority desires to know "Truth", many remain reluctant to read the Bible.

Perhaps you are one who has tried to read the Bible, but it just got too confusing so you turned it away. Or perhaps you've had a negative experience with "religion" so you abandoned it all together. I wouldn't be surprised if some of you have seen a friend or a loved one "become religious"; then they went around condemning others (that don't believe as they do). I myself am baffled how a "believer" could go about telling another *that they're going to hell,* when they claim to be a believer of **"judge not or ye be judged",** unfortunately hypocrisy is not uncommon among religions. However, this book is not about religions or even "becoming religious", it is solely about **TRUTH.**

This book is especially designed for those who have picked up the Bible but for some reason they lost interest. I can understand if one made it halfway through the Book of Exodus, and none of it seemed to make any sense. The Bible is unlike other books, it is a collection of stories written by several different authors, to read it from the beginning to end, can easily put one in a state of confusion. For the "Old Testament" is filled with story after story of God telling us to do "this" we say, "yes" but then we *don't do it* and God punishes us. What we need to realize is that the "Old Testament" is only the "First Act", the stories are meant to teach us "how hopelessly lost we all are", so that when the "Truth" comes in the "New Testament" we understand our desperate need for salvation. It is the "Old Testament" that prepares the world for the "Good News".

9

This book is dedicated to those who
SEEK TRUTH.

"Why does God allow so much pain and suffering?"
An angel is asked and responds in such,
"You are asking for wisdom, you are not ready to hear".
"Try me", the question remains.
The angel reluctantly answers:
"Satan is the prince of this (material) world.
Everything around you, even this body, is a distraction to
hide you from **the Truth**. You are not flesh, you are spirit,
but thinking that this is your life, you cling to it,
not understanding it is but a distraction.
The Truth is, you are richly blessed to live in a world with
suffering, you're blessed because you have the opportunity
to respond with charity and forgiveness, thus praising God.
But your desire, is for that of revenge, taking back, I
ask *does taking back from them or harming them
ever give it back to you or ease your suffering?*
No, nor will it ever.
Justice does not exist within *your realm.*
The greatest blessing God has bestowed unto you is **Faith**.
You can **BELIEVE**, you can **praise God** without
knowing... I am in awe, over the opportunity
you have to glorify the LORD, for there
is no greater gift in all of heaven.
If you can only (pauses), if you only hear one thing I say,
let this be it, *your brief moment here, is your one and
only time, that will forever determine your eternity.*
Use it wisely.
Love with all your strength and all your heart,
desperately seek to forgive those who have harmed you and
then, not only will you receive *peace* in this world, but
treasures so great in heaven, you are not even capable
of fathoming... (Shakes his head) I say to you, this
worlds *suffering*, is not worthy of being compared,
to the glory which will be revealed,
to those who **BELIEVE**."

11

Understand that you do not understand,
so that you may begin to understand.

~

God measures your worth in humbleness.

~

The moment you realize, you are a Fool,
you gain much wisdom.

~

It is not within reason to think *there is no Creator*,
unless there was no existence.

~

Forgiveness, Charity, Healing, Hope, Faith...
None of these exist in Heaven.
There's no Forgiveness, because in Heaven
there is no longer Sin.
There's no Charity, because in Heaven
there is no longer Suffering.
There's no Healing, because in Heaven
there is no longer Pain.
There's no Hope, because in Heaven
you abide with God.
There's no Faith, because in Heaven
you know God.

~

Avoid the illusion of knowing.
The false perception of knowing,
suppresses the will to learn more.

~

Seek truth, even when surrounded by lies.

"EXPENSIVE" Religious decor
is only displayed by *hypocrites*, for if they truly
believed in that which the decoration represented,
they would sell it and give that money to the poor.
For instance: Take a very expensive **gold cross**
necklace or better yet one with **diamonds**, has
it not become *common place* for people to
wear such **expensive jewelry, as a way**
to display their *love for* or *honor for* **Jesus**?
Yet **lavish material** completely opposes
everything Jesus stands for.
Who is Jesus?
Is He not **meek, humble, giving, caring...**
How is it then, that we have beguiled ourselves into
adorning our churches, our homes, even *our necks* with
extravagant material, as a way of displaying our faith?
*If you truly believe in Jesus, sell your religious valuables
and give that money to the poor, the needy, then
you will truly be honoring Jesus.*
Through the SPIRIT.

~

Seek to destroy and you already have.

~

Parents: Imagine if you will, your children as fish,
and it is your job to provide them with a current,
leading them in the right direction, so if later
they ever decide to go the wrong way, they
would have to swim against the current.

~

The best way to fix a problem in society,
is to find the feed line to its roots,
then change its diet.

If you appear righteous in the sight of men,
but foul in the sight of God,
What do you have?
If you appear righteous in the sight of God,
but foul in the sight of men,
What are you missing?

~

Find comfort in knowing that:
If this was a *perfect world*, you would not be in it.
Don't take it personally that goes for everybody.

~

If you get angered by what others say about you,
then it should be true.
For why would you ever bother getting angry, *if it was not?*

~

Parents HUG your Children!
It's not enough, just tell them that you love them,
they need to feel it.
Being held in a loving embrace is **SO IMPORTANT**,
that the need for it,
is distilled in us *at birth*.
Babies cry for three reasons,
Changing, Feeding, and to be Held.
I promise, you will **never regret**
making your child,
feel LOVED.

~

Children are on their best behavior when their father
is in the room, for fear of punishment. But if the
father leaves, then secretly watches his children,
he will soon discover their true behavior.

The wise understand
that everything they own is on temporary loan and that
possessions are merely an illusion. For no one can take any
earthly possession with him or her when they die. Surely
they may *possess* a possession for a little while, but sooner
or later "it will come to pass", that every *thing* will be left
behind. In spite of that, understand that when you die, you
actually take with you *more than you can imagine and
more real than any tangible thing you ever possessed.*
Because the Truth is, everything that is "intangible"
will last and endure forever.
Do not believe with your eyes,
nor believe in what you can *touch*,
for both are no more than deceptions.
Permanence only exists in the intangible truths of being.
All materials (including your body) will inevitably decay.
Thus, no one can keep a possession forever. But, the
act of giving a material possession is eternal, for
no matter what happens to that given object
the act, has been placed within eternity.
So in TRUTH, only that which *you*
give, is what you *keep forever.*

~

A man was walking into a store
when a lady approached him for money
"Help me, my son is sick, he may be dying
and I have no money to buy him any medicine",
the man kindly gave the woman a twenty dollar bill.
Shortly after, some people told him "you shouldn't
give that woman any money, she's out there every
day with new lies, to try to get people's money".
He asked, "You mean she doesn't have an ill son?"
"No", they replied.
"That's great", the man answered back.

If you had a vegetable garden and some of your plants
were not producing well, would you nourish and care
for them more, or pick them out and plant new ones?
Beware...

~

I find it interesting how the conscience only bothers
good people, but they have to do something bad first.

~

To love those who love you is good,
and to love those who only like you is better,
but to love even those who *despise you*, is the best.

~

Do you want to know TRUTH?
You may think you do,
but if you really did, you would know Him already.

~

Competition with others *belittles you,*
beating others should not make you feel better
about yourself. For true competition comes from within.
Strive only to reach your maximum potential, for this
accomplishment far surpasses all other awards.

~

When someone close to you dies
you do not feel sad for them,
you feel sad for yourself
because it hurts you,
to be without them.

~

You should rather wound yourself than strike another.

Everything that is good in me,
comes from God working through me.

~

Do not feed a flower poison then expect it to bloom.

~

To reach a destination
you must fulfill **all** the steps to get there.
If you only travel ninety-nine percent of the way,
the only thing you have accomplished is a great view.

~

New encounters, begin with an instinct
either negative or positive.
To think you *will* or *will not* like something,
sways you towards that judgment.
For this reason, many people have liked you,
not because of you, but simply because they wanted to,
and that also goes vice-a-versa.

~

If you were to weigh in comparison the amount of time in
life, to that of death, one of them would be so light,
it would not even register on the scale. Yet it
is that *nil time*, we concern ourselves over.

~

Humbleness is not putting your self down,
it is simply placing God before you.

~

Do not accept what you hear *about God*,
unless you first find it *true* within yourself,
for many who *speak of God*, do not know *Him*.

Some of the *highest scholars* are clueless,
some of the *religious leaders* are unholy,
and some of the politicians are honest.
Do not respect or disrespect a profession,
but rather the **Character of the Individual.**

~

Know *Thy God.*

~

Do you think it's easier for one
to die for their beliefs, or to live by them?

~

When I was young, a loud obnoxious man
explained to me, how drugs *never* affected him.
I knew right then, I would never do drugs.

~

God lives in everyone,
yet we constantly insist on living for ourselves.

~

There is no value in material.
Only in Generosity

~

God not only knows,
what you're thinking now,
He knows what you will be thinking in the future.

~

Pray not only for those who *are loving*,
for they know God, but pray for those who are *unloving*,
for they need prayer the most.

I see God as...

_____

_____

_____

_____

_____

_____

_____

Take a moment to Thank God for blessing you with...

_____

_____

_____

_____

_____

_____

_____

"TRUE DECEPTION"

Here a man and the Deceiver
are sitting at a park bench
with a chess game between them:

DECEIVER
"Do you play?
I've always found a great fault with this game.
It's all these useless pawns, good for nothing but
getting in the way or sacrificing. Ha, course the biggest
joke is their impotent king who's what, slightly better than
that *of one single pawn* (shakes his head in disgust).
Now this (touches the queen piece), this is the true power,
able to move forth in all directions, near or far,
obviously the superior piece on the board.
This should be the leader.
What do you think?"

MAN
"What do you want"?

DECIEVER
"What belongs to me".

MAN
"What do you want with me"?

DECIEVER
"I just want to talk, tell you a little about myself,
cause I know you're scared but if you were smarter
you'd be terrified.
You have no idea what I'm capable of.
Your kind, you're so pathetic and weak. I could tell you
everything and you still wouldn't get it (he smiles).

20

If it wasn't for the extreme pleasure it brings me,
to rip your kind away from God, I wouldn't even
bother wasting my time with filth like you.
You're nothing.
I'm the exalted one. I alone am worthy.
I've made men hate, because they want *others* to live in
love. I have made people commit murder, to prove they're
against killing. I've made people condemn loved ones, tell
them they're going to hell (continues in a whisper) simply
because they don't share the same point of view.
I have falsified the whole world.
And I do it through
D E C E P T I O N
Course Temptations and Lies have always been good to me
but to make men do evil while believing they're doing
good, just goes to prove, what a **LAME creation** you are.
You would at least be somewhat wise if you just had a clue,
of just how enormously ignorant you truly are. But you
go around worshiping me and you don't even realize it.
You're pathetic.
Anything, that you don't put God *first in*,
makes me the ruler of, and let me tell you
MY KINGDOM IS VAST!
Hell, I love how most people don't even bother to seek
God. I've got you so wrapped up in your petty desires that
you forsake just about everything that matters, ha, ha.
You're nothing more than maggots. You know one of my
favorite ways to pass time, is beguiling those who truly
want to *be holy* (he says with disgust), and *seek God.*
YOU COULDN'T EVEN BEGIN TO FATHOM
THE HORRORS I'VE MADE MEN DO
FOR THE LOVE OF GOD.
And that's TRUE DECEPTION.
Ha, ha, ha, and let me tell you,
nothing makes for a more devout killer than *Religion.*"

MAN
"I don't believe you."

DECEIVER
**"Have not more *wars* been started, people killed,
families divided, over religion than all else combined?**
All I have to do is tantalize different faiths, that *they* belong
to the true side of God, and that it is but *God's will* that
they kill the disbelievers, then just sit back and watch as
they start to persecute, hate, and kill each other. BANG!
(He shoots with his fingers)
BANG! BANG! BANG! BANG! BANG!
Oh… it' beautiful.
Pathetic part is that most of you don't *believe* in your
religion cause it's true, you make it true **because you
believe it.** I mean come on now, some of the things your
kind believes, granted you're incredibly mentally deficient,
but DAMN! You make it too easy.
Your *kind* love's being right, more than it love's God,
combine that with your love of making choices
out of ignorance and you got what I call
'THE WAY OF MAN'.
Hey, if anything here is upsetting you, then it must be true,
cause I couldn't imagine you getting worked up, over
oimplo, diomiooiblo, littlo lioo. Now of oouroo, I'm tolling
you this, knowing nothing's going to stick. Sure you may
want to change, ha, perhaps even try, but sooner or later
I will get you back, cause everywhere you look you'll
see *me*. I am in pride, lust, *love of money*, greed…
I am everywhere and **GOD…** Where is He?
There has only been one, ONE who fully
denied *his own will* for the *will of God*.
JUST ONE!
(The devil looks up towards heaven and screams)
I AM THE PRINCE OF THIS WORLD!!!"

22

A wise person loves to be corrected,
when they are guided (through patience and kindness),
to understand the error in their ways. Whereas the
unwise person tends to be short tempered,
and sometimes even becomes hostile.

~

Ignorance is the essence of evil.
Evildoers know not, whom they truly harm.

~

Wisdom comes from - **Understanding** - comes from Love.

~

Great humility is a sign of tremendous wisdom.

~

Know that you are not the same as you were yesterday,
nor will you be the same tomorrow.
Every second is an opportunity for you to make a change.

~

God blesses parents with babies,
so that they could experience a glimpse
of the love that He has for them.

~

The *cup of desire*
has a big hole at the bottom,
no matter how much you put into it,
it will always require just a little more.

~

God made all of us like a rainbow,
colorful and beautiful when we shine.

Deeper love comes to those who are willing to lose.

~

Enlightenment comes from dimming yourself,
so that God's light can shine through you.

~

Scripture is best understood
through the light of other scripture.

~

Success in life is dependant upon a viewpoint,
the question to ask yourself is who's.

~

If everyone, everywhere, were to combine all that they
know, it would still be nothing in comparison to
what is capable of being known.

~

If you know me, you may not love me,
but if you know God, then you love me.
Because to truly know God, is to love everyone.

~

Beliefs form thoughts,
thoughts direct our actions, actions portray our character.
Look at your actions
and you will discover what you truly believe.

~

Be slow with others, for those who are *good*, are only good
mostly and those who are *bad*, are only bad mostly.
And within a short amount of time, you will
not know, which they truly are.

A truth about giving:
Those who only give what they do not want or need,
give very little and those who give that of which
they treasure or hold dearest, give the most.
The dollar value is less significant to
the value of which you hold on it,
for true giving comes
from sacrifice.

~

If children are the future, then the elderly are the past
and the middle aged would be the present.
On the contrary,
the truth is we are *all* just as much an imprint of the past,
an influence on the present and the hope for the future.

~

The best advice I could give another, is to pray
and truly listen, then God will advise from within.

~

Life is not merited by achievements or personal gain,
but only through acts of kindness and generosity.

~

A wise man is no different than a fool,
other than he has become aware
of his own foolishness.

~

Grief over a broken heart is a great compliment to yourself,
for many people have never loved deeply enough to suffer.

~

One who thinks *they know it all*, learns nothing.

Portray compassion as the rainbow portrays color.
Desire righteousness as the fish desires water.
Shine with kindness as the sun shines bright.
Long for charity as birds long for flight.
Be forgiving as the seed is fruitful.
Love one another as God loves you.

~

If you hate those
who embellish within sinfulness, then you deny Love.
But if you Love those
who embellish within the sinfulness that you hate,
then they always have a door of compassion
left open before them.

~

You cannot teach:
The desire to learn, the caring for others, the longing
to improve oneself, the joys of life, the love of tasks,
the appreciation of beauty, or the appetite of spirit.
You must first desire these for yourself.
For if you seek, you will find.

~

Love those who think differently than you.
Hear me, love those who think differently and if they
persecute you, deliver only kindness upon them.

~

It is easy to remain afloat on calm waters.

~

Look at people and really listen to your thoughts about
them,
and you will learn a great deal about yourself.

It is just as easy to worry, as it is to smile,
the only difference is *one makes you feel better*.

~

Why become one? This separates you from the many,
instead become all, then you won't leave out any.

~

The more you have, the harder it becomes to give.
Many people have beguiled themselves into thinking,
that they will give more, only when they have more.

~

Those who are wise, rejoice
for you will always have what matters most.

~

Finding the good in a person instead of the bad,
makes both of you better people.

~

Bad situations require the best of you, not the worst.

~

Pray not what God can do for you,
but what *you* can do for God.

~

Words do not move people,
it is the individuals comprehension,
then the thoughts derived upon this comprehension,
that moves a person.

~

To grow in love, you must wither in hate.

Keep in mind, those who *deserve* to be loved the least,
likely have received the least love.

~

Any time you think badly upon another,
you harm only yourself.

~

Holy people are simply those who love ALL.

~

One who professes virtues and beliefs that
they do not possess, is worse than one who
blatantly admits their wickedness.

~

It is only through the testing of faith
that a person uncovers how much they truly believe.
For no one knows the integrity of a tree until it is tested.
When harsh winds blow, the trees that have weak roots fall
and those with deep roots withstand mighty winds.

~

Question that of which is *believed to be known*,
many great new things are discovered this way.

~

Think about a family member or a friend
that you deeply love. Now take a moment and really think
about how much you love that person. Have you ever
looked at that person in awe, completely amazed
by how much you love them?
God loves us even more than that!
Because we are imperfect, and God's love is perfect,
His love greatly exceeds what we are even capable of.

A man once complained that he had no shoes, till one passed who had no legs. Be grateful for what you have, even when you *think* you have very little.

~

The greatest teachers are those who promote the joy of learning to their students.

~

The best way to tell somebody something, is to earnestly listen to them.

~

Put this book down and go give somebody a HUG.

~

Money is nothing more than an opportunity to do good or evil.

~

The *body* requires nourishment to develop, as does the *mind*, as does the *spirit*.
Food tones to the body.
Interaction tones to the mind.
Love tones to the spirit.

~

Suffering of the flesh is inevitable, it will die. Notice I say *it*, not you.

~

The **soul** is the only substantial element of life.

~

Seek not only to find but find it in yourself TO SEEK.

There's only one kind of person in this world, YOU.
How you perceive others is merely a form of yourself.

~

There is one eternal **Law**,
one eternal l**O**ve,
one eternal wo**R**d,
one eternal ju**D**ge.

~

We are not even capable of fathoming, what is possible!
What we now find *impossible* becomes the *next possible*
and with those achievements, we will thus create
a new *batch of impossible*.

~

Only a disillusioned person could ever conceive that
"their words" brought a person to believe in Christ,
for glory and honor belong to God and God alone.

~

Experience; simply means one has tried it before,
not that they are more intelligent, enthusiastic,
passionate, or capable, than one who has yet to try.

If you find it difficult to appreciate what you have,
chop off one of your arms. I assure you afterwards you
would be quite satisfied with just having that arm back. For
those who are not satisfied with what they have, will never
be satisfied with having more but most likely they will
miss something the moment it has been taken away.

~

Freedom is an act of responsibility.

30

Everyone has their own personal level of comprehension;
Therefore communication is best achieved when
comprehension levels are closely aligned.
Thus creating a mutually beneficial platform
for both parties to convey and understand the other.

~

Time has no existence *within itself* because it is eternal,
it has neither a beginning or an end.
Thus, no reference could be taken to differentiate one
moment from another.
An *action* must occur to establish an existence of time.
Thus, a *time* is a given placement of *an action.*
For actions create placements, these placements create an
order of distinction, and it is the *distance between* these
distinctions that we have come to *represent* as time.
What is the past, but a frozen moment of action?
Time is a place.

~

Technology does not improve humanity.
It is only through our increase in the assistance of others,
that humanity improves.

~

What is your true desire for wanting a tomorrow?
Make this a priority for today.

~

Speak not when you know but ask when you do not.
Only by asking questions can we increase our knowledge.

~

The question *within the question*
is what one should answer, not the question itself.

Two thirsty men were each digging for a well.
One man dug with all his determination and focus on
reaching his goal, while the other man dug with just as
much effort, he took a moment to reflect on his course of
action. It was during this time that he noticed a river
nearby. Sometimes those who appear the busiest
are merely wasting time.

~

Regrets are one of the best learning experiences,
because they are often the most painful.

~

Parents:
When your children behave badly,
think back to the time when you behaved so to your
parents, then before you react ask yourself "do I want
my child to experience this kind of memory
or perhaps another?"

~

The essence of your spirit,
is an everlasting embodiment of all the deeds of your heart.

~

As a fruit tree;
Your *thoughts* would be the soil.
Your *actions* would be the tree.
And your *intentions* are the fruit.

~

Your state of mind
relinquishes corresponding emotions.
Therefore when you feel an unwanted or unpleasant
emotion, quickly think about something else.

Look upon the faults of others
as a chance to amend *your own*.

~

You understand
will not while you this read to remember line.
That sentence makes no sense, but you dwell over it.
Why?
Because your mind desires a *classification* so that the
information can be stored, processed and later forgotten.
Free yourself from this ludicrous mentality.
Desire not order, but *substance*.
For what is remembered
that which is said, or what is understood?

~

Past, Present, and Future,
were all created at the *same time*, they coexist as one.
Take one away and all three would cease to exist.

~

Since childhood we have been trained that learning
is derived upon *memorization*.
Why?
Time passes and we simply forget.
School should rather stimulate curiosity & expand the
imagination, for that creates lasting education.

~

Material desires are like that of a thirsty man
swimming in the middle of the ocean.
Yet
spiritual gifts are like that of a farmer who plows and
sows, and at the end of the day, *appears* to
have nothing to show for it.

My Top 5 Priorities in Life are...

1. _____

2. _____

3. _____

4. _____

5. _____

I Spend Most of My Time...

_____

_____

_____

_____

_____

Five ways I can improve myself...

1. _____

2. _____

3. _____

4. _____

5. _____

34

I once saw a beautiful painting of Jesus.
Oh, it was so beautiful, it cost a few hundred dollars, but I
had to have it. The painting would look so great in my
home and I could proudly display my faith to
everyone who entered my home. But
God spoke to my heart and said
That I should not buy it,
I was completely perplexed.
This painting was amazing; I *tried* explaining myself to
God, *that I only wanted to display my faith* and
God replied *then go give the money that you would buy this
painting with, and give it to the poor and the needy.*
What???
Wait a minute, aren't I trying to do something good here?
I mean it's a Christian painting, in a Christian store.
I don't understand.
Then God said, "if you truly want to show me your faith,
YOU WILL GIVE."
What do I say to that? I must have stood in front of that
painting for what seemed like an hour. *But, I knew
God was right.* For God is spirit and we are to
worship him IN SPIRIT.

~

How you say, matters twice over what you say.

~

It is the impermanence of all things
that magnifies our appreciation for all things.

~

If I were to spel this sintance incorectly,
wood peeple stil understand it?
So what then is the significance of speling
or grammar, to comprehending?

35

Free your mind from focusing on non-essentials.
Many people overlook the entire message
by focusing on *a minute detail.*

~

You know what makes your favorite, *your favorite?*
All the others.

~

What is remembered becomes forgotten.
What is experienced through emotion becomes you.
Experience the study.

~

You may love one others dislike,
just as you may dislike one others love.
Though which of these is
the true representation
of that individual?
They are *both* an experience of that individual.

~

Can you name one sin that you are not guilty of?

~

When you pass on,
which would you rather be remembered for?
Being beautiful. Being rich. Being smart. Being kind.
Only **one** promotes a sense of true loss.

~

Peace comes freely, yet destructive emotions require effort.

~

Never waste your time talking about…

36

**It is better to belong to a "wrong religion"
and love everyone,
than belong to the "right religion"
and hate anyone.**

*"Dear friends, let us love one another,
for love comes from God.
Everyone who loves
has been born of God and knows God.
Whoever does not love does not know God,
because God is love. This is how God showed His
love among us: He sent his one and only Son into the
world that we might live through him.
This is love: not that we loved God, but that He loved
us and sent His Son as an atoning
sacrifice for our sins.
Dear friends,
since God so loved us,
we also ought to love one another.
No one has ever seen God; but if we love one another,
God lives in us and His love is made complete in us...
We love because He first loved us.*
**If anyone says, "I love God," yet hates his brother,
he is a liar.**
*For anyone who does not love his brother,
whom he has seen, cannot love God,
whom he has not seen.
And He has given us this command:
Whoever loves God must also love his brother."*
(1 John 4:7-20)

If you want someone to remember what you say,
it is best to *evoke an emotion* within them.
Then give them a chance to mentally
respond by speaking freely.
Their mind will have a great need to transform your speech
towards their way of speaking.
Then it's no longer your speech, but theirs.

~

That which **"is"**,
is only understood by us, through comparing its similar
and/or contrary traits with others. For to fully comprehend
what something **"is"**, is to also comprehend *what it is not.*

~

The best way to debate with a person
is by *completely agreeing* with them first.
By agreeing, you cancel out all their
ammunition for argument.
Then their focus is no longer on retaliation, but listening.

~

To call it you name it. To name it you label it.
To label it you restrict it. To restrict it is to deny its truth.
God answers His name to Moses as "I AM"
For God is without limits.

~

Ignorant people never know that they are,
so take my advice and *know that you are ignorant,*
so that you could no longer possibly be.

~

We've killed many of the greatest minds, we cherish today.
What does this tell us about our understanding?

Knowing often hinders the expansion of the mind,
for the *perils of knowledge* are infinite.
To think you know puts an end towards further
understanding, rather realize, that your
belief of knowing, is no more than
your perception thus far.

~

Order of Creation:
Existence
Awareness
Conscience
Freedom
Behavior
Placement

~

Nourishing regret is like planting a rock, neither produce.

~

Money cannot create *eternal fortune*, only generosity.

~

One who finds acceptance within,
needs not the acceptance of others. And
one who needs the acceptance of others,
has yet to find acceptance within.

~

You are to me, as I see you to be.
I am to you, as you see me to be.

~

We are born with a vast wisdom
that gradually becomes limited to soothe *our self.*

God has given you a temple in your body, seek not to defile
it with impurities of this world but tend to it as the
blessing it is. For how you treat what God has
given you is a *reflection* of your
gratitude and faith.

~

When a loved one dies, it is very common
to become engulfed in grief, confusion,
and perhaps sometimes even anger.
All of these emotions create that which they represent
but one could also choose to cherish all the fond
memories that were shared with that person,
give thanks to God for the time that they
did get with their loved one, and find
comfort in understanding that they
are not "truly dead", but have
simply passed on to a place
where one day they can
be reunited forever.
Emotions rely on one's view of death.
How one copes with death is a testimony to ones faith.

~

The thought of giving is like digging a hole to plant a tree,
both are necessary, but remain empty till fulfilled.

~

Not so long ago, I heard about a young girl who was
shot and killed, while she was praying. I then
overheard one say "how could there be
a God that would let such a
horrible thing happen?"
When all that was going through my mind was
Wow! What a tremendous way to die.

True religion loves all.
True religion is accepting.
True religion is a way of life.
True religion always cares for others.
True religion refuses to let the world corrupt us.

~

Love all who are good,
and all those who have a huge potential
for being good (which we call bad).

~

Which is larger Infinity or Infinity?
They are equal,
and yet "Infinity" exists within a marble
just as much as it does *within a much larger planet.*
For anything, of any size, could infinitely be split in half.

~

You are unaware of, *that to* which you are aware of.
Thus the only true awareness exists within
the state of *awareness of unawareness.*

~

If you want to change something about yourself,
act as if you already have.
And instantaneously you will.

~

Sex and Money are similar
they can either a blessing or a sin.

~

The only thing one would could possibly conceive about
Infinity, is their inability to conceive infinity.

Fictional Story:
A plane was about to crash, inside were many religious leaders of the world, the airline steward quickly gathered them all together and gave each of them a parachute. The steward then instructed them that the Rabbi would jump first, followed by the Catholic Priest, the Hindu, the Muslim, the Buddhist, and at the very end of the line was the Christian. Overcome by curiosity the Christian had to ask "Why did you put me last". The steward replied, "Well because I also believe in Jesus and he taught us *to treat others the way we would want to be treated,* right?" Christian answered "yes", but was still not quite following. Seeing the confused expression the steward quickly explained further "You see I know I desperately want to get off this plane, ASAP so I treated them the way I would have wanted to be treated."

~

All good deeds are nullified through boasting.

~

It is better to give *an ounce of kindness,*
than it is to receive *a vast amount of knowledge.*

~

The foolish mistake wisdom
for that which they *desire* to be true.

~

Purity of the soul is love.

~

If you don't enjoy giving,
you're missing out on one of the greatest
blessings in giving.

(An angel speaks about God)
"You get to lead a life without ever knowing God truly exists *until you die*. You get to **choose** whether to believe or not believe (shakes his head in the sheer awe).
For I was created knowing God. I have dwelled in His heavenly kingdom, with all of God's glory radiating upon me. I... there was never a question of *does God exist* for I KNOW. But you, you are beyond blessed, with something I never had,
<u>YOU CAN BELIEVE.</u>
Believe with all your heart, without knowing, without...
IT IMPRESSES ME,
HOW MUCH
GOD HAS GIVEN YOU.
To believe without knowing is the ultimate praise."

~

Before I tell you **something** that is wrong in you, please allow me a few days to tell you *some of the things* that are wrong with me.

~

A man once noticed a blind man and a deaf man standing nearby, he wanted to do something to help them improve their way of life, so he decided to take them both to a nearby shop and he explained to each of them, that he would buy them anything in the whole store. He was utterly baffled when the blind man exited the store with a beautiful painting of a sunset and the deaf man exited the store with a finely crafted harmonica, for the blind man could surely not appreciate the artistry and the deaf man could not enjoy the music. The man dwelled over this a great deal. He just couldn't comprehend *WHY?* Then it dawned on him, a lot of people focus on what *they WISH they had*, rather than making the most of what *they DO have*.

What if...

I once thought to myself what a horror it would be *IF* after death, I had to constantly view my life over and over again as some kind of ghostly spectator. Because I know I have (more often than not), become subdued by the *so-called heavy burdens, conflicts, and toils of everyday life.* I would see myself going to work all day then coming home and when my children say they want to play with me, I would reply "I'm too tired". I would see myself strive for a certain luxurious lifestyle only to increase it every time it was achieved. I would see moments after moments misused. "How could I have possibly been so naive?" would ring through my mind. I would see myself casually departing from friends or family not knowing that it would be the last moment I will ever spend with them. I would *sigh* watching all of this in a despairing state, denying through and through that *this* could have ever been me. **If** I could only just tell myself one thing, I would tell myself "LOVE MORE" because you just don't realize how little time you have, till you're just about all out.

~

The fastest way to get from one place to another,
is to change your perspective.

~

We as a society constantly bring each other down
by continuously leading one another
towards what we have mislabeled as up.

~

The depths of wisdom embrace the surface of love.

~

The plagues of humanity *are mere symptoms of ignorance.*

44

Yad lla tuoba kniht uoy tahw uoy gnitteg no skrow
dnim suoisnocbus ruoy.

~

I feel that mankind in some way desires separation.
Look at <u>racism</u>, for example. How infallibly <u>pathetic</u>
of a reason to discredit another individual than that of
their skin tone. Yet by doing so look at what is achieved,
a <u>superiority complex, an enemy to smack down and raise</u>
<u>levels of self esteem, and an immediate *family* of belonging</u>
(these are some of the reasons kids join gangs). That sense,
that need for *belonging* is so strong, so important, that we
have for centuries now inflicted hate, violence, and
suffering just to sustain it.
All for the false notion that we are different, because "if"
one can establish a *difference*, then and only then
could one be *better*.
Why do we not live in peace?
Because peace brings unity, which carries <u>no pride,</u>
<u>nor the euphoria of dominance, nor conflicts (which</u>
<u>create opportunities for triumph), it doesn't carry an</u>
<u>immediate acceptance into a physical classification,</u>
<u>or a particular fellowship, or a camaraderie, or</u>
instant *"friends"*, that can unite themselves
over the smacking down of mutual *enemies*,
thus raising levels of self worth. You
see with *peace* there is no thrill
OF BOOSTING ONES EGO.
Peace requires **courage, and the strength** to stand on one's
own and believe in
themselves.
Peace demands True Character.

~

Do not tell me who you are, **live so that I may know.**

45

Death does not separate us from loved ones,
it creates an everlasting unification of our heart and soul.

~

What is read is no longer what was written
but transforms from *itself*,
to the readers personal interpretation of what was written.

~

At one time or another,
I have taken for granted every single blessing God has ever
given me. Yet every single day He gives me more.
How marvelous and generous our God is.

~

With everyone and *every living thing* that God created in
the world, are you Significant to God?
Hear me,
you are most <u>precious</u> in the eye's of God.
God made you absolutely *unique* and extremely special.
And He made you for one reason, **for His pleasure,**
because <u>He desires for us to know **Him**</u>
and it pleases HIm greatly to share
His love with you.

~

We receive *death* through the gift of life,
and we receive *true life* through a gift of death.

~

People once believed that the world was flat, this was a
logical assessment considering that's *how one sees it*
but over time we have come to learn that there is
more to the world than *just what we see.*

God is not found in a church or a temple,
He is only found in the heart.

~

Personally:
I don't believe in Jesus
because he paid the price for my sins.
I don't believe in Jesus
because he came back from the dead.
I don't believe in Jesus
because of his many, many, many miracles.
I BELIEVE IN JESUS
just because of what he taught.
Love that immense could only come **from God.**

~

Some people are
Pro-Choice and against *Capital Punishment*
This simply means that
they believe it is "Just" to:
Kill an Innocent Life
and
Spare the Life of a Convicted Murderer.

~

Wars killed many, Bombs killed many,
Guns killed many, Swords killed many,
Arrows killed many, Abortion killed all.

~

If you are convicted by your sins,
REPENT (seek God's forgiveness and turn from your sin).
If you are sincere (and God knows your heart), **He will
forgive you,** by the measure that you forgive those
who have sinned against you.

47

I Believe Jesus is...

_____

_____

_____

_____

_____

_____

**If You were Saved by Works,
Which would You Submit to God?**

_____

_____

_____

_____

_____

_____

_____

_____

Are you willing to **die** for what you believe?
If so, then you truly believe.
Are you willing to **kill** for what you believe?
If so, then evil has a tight grasp on you.

~

You are never doing God's will, by hating another.
NEVER!
What if they are *sinners*?
My friend, who do you think you are?
WE ARE ALL SINNERS.
Don't think for a second, that I'm telling you to love *sin*,
HATE the **SIN** a person does,
but always **LOVE** the **SINNER**.

~

Believers usually believe their religion is the one true
divine faith and with well over a hundred various religions,
there's a whole lot of wrong people out there.
So even when you can't agree,
you should always be
Loving and
Kind.

~

Could God forgive even a GREAT sinner?
Heaven rejoices more over one sinner, who repents,
than 99 who remain *righteous*.

~

Faith is being less concerned with *your own problems*
and more compassionate towards other peoples.

~

Let go of regrets, so that you can reach out for joy.

49

It's human nature to want to
hurt someone who has hurt you,
but God desire's that you forgive.
It's human nature to be selfish,
but God desire's that you love one another.
It's human nature to love those, who love you,
but God desire's that you love even those who hate you.
It is human nature to desire recognition, when one gives,
but God desire's that you give in secret.
It is human nature for us to crave material items,
but God desire's that you store up treasures in heaven.
It is human nature to want to be exalted,
but God desire's that you humble yourself.
It is human nature to sin,
but God desire's that you repent.
In every way,
God's *nature* far exceeds human *desire*.

~

The only *sure thing* there is in gambling is *to not bet at all.*
And being the betting man that I am,
I always bet on sure things.

~

Most of us spend our life just trying to fit in
Yet ironically, the ones we tend to admire and talk about
the most are the ones who standout.

~

Some people get so angered
by the *accusation* that they live in hate,
that they kill the person who said it.

~

Just so you know, *God's watching you right now.*

**If everything was created by God,
then *Who* created God?**

Based solely on *man's keen intellect,*
one would have to submit that in order to
have **a Creation** there must be **a Creator.**
And being that YOU are a **Creation**, you must therefore
be inclined to acknowledge, the existence of a **Creator.**
So we have established that there is "A Creator".

But with regards to **The Creator of All** a dilemma arises,
the Creator of All could not possibly have been created,
for if *He* was, then *He* couldn't be
"The Creator of All".
Being such,
there's only two possibilities for the concept of
THE CREATOR OF ALL

First being that
The Creator of All
(otherwise known as "**God**")
Simply doesn't exist.

Second is,
that **God, the Creator of All** does exist
has always existed and will forever continue
to exist, completely Self Sufficient, All Knowledgeable,
All Powerful, Without Limits, and even (get this),
even able to surpass man's severely
limited ability to reason.

Personally:
I have seen the intelligence of man and I'm not impressed,
but when I look up at an evening sky and see the stars
and the vastness of space, I'm in awe.

51

GOD WILL PROVIDE

Abraham was "one of the greatest *Men of Faith*".
His faith in God was so great, that when God told him to
take his son to the region of *Moriah* and offer him as a
sacrifice. Abraham obeyed and took his son up to a
mountain top and with the help of his son, they
set up a sacrificial altar. When the son asked
his father *where is the sacrifice that they
are going to kill,* the father had to look
into his loving sons eyes and reply
YOU ARE, MY SON.
Now the son should have naturally been overcome with
tremendous fear and grief but the son obeyed his father's
will and offered himself freely. Just before Abraham was
about to sacrifice his son, God (being pleased by faith)
stopped him and then richly rewarded him. The son
who was then saved, asked his father *what shall
they do with the altar that they just made* and
Abraham proclaimed that **The LORD Will Provide.**
Years later in that same region the Lord did provide,
(only this time it was God's son)
J E S U S   C H R I S T

~

Good deeds are but filthy rags in the eyes of God,
but on the same token,
they act as a *testimony* to ones faith.
For deeds are a reflection of faith and faith is great in the
eyes of God. So seek to live by faith and produce as many
good deeds as you can, because faith is a reflection of the
sum of your deeds. As faith without deeds is dead, faith
with many deeds is alive. It is by the *Wisdom of God*,
that we are not saved by *our deeds,* lest any man
should boast, for boasting produces *pride*, the
consuming sin, that caused an angel to fall.

Americans imagine if one day,
Aliens landed their ships on America, in order to start a new colony, one based on peace, freedom, and prosperity. Now the aliens had no idea how the American people would respond, for they had never seen an American before. Most Americans responded in awe and kindness. So the aliens befriended the American people but shortly after, the aliens thought of themselves far superior to the Americans and being that these ungodly savages consumed their new homeland, the aliens thought it best to kill most of the Americans and enslave the rest, they were all but wiped out, soon the alien race changed their mind and their policies, so they decided to let the Americans live as *free men*, bearing that they did so in the areas selected by the aliens. All this, built the foundation for a beautiful alien culture that thrived and prospered for many centuries, some even came to call it "the greatest nation in the world", being that they were one nation under God and stood for liberty and justice for all.
Incidentally this story works just as well if you replace the word "Americans" with *Indians* and the word "Aliens" with *our ancestors*.

~

Christians:
Do not put your faith in "Christianity",
put all your faith in **Jesus**.

~

God speaks through the silence of our heart.

~

Instead of longing for something
you don't have, try spending an entire day
appreciating everything that you do have.

53

Jesus told us to be Humble
yet many Christians exalt themselves.
Jesus told us to Judge Not
yet many Christians judge others.
Jesus told us to be Giving
yet many Christians think of themselves.
Jesus told us to Forgive
yet many Christians condemn others.
Jesus told us to Love
yet many Christians hate.
Christians are in no way perfect,
only Jesus is perfect.
Therefore,
Put your faith in Jesus alone, not the
community of sinners that are
known as *Christians.*
~

If you were a farmer and had a grand apple tree
(perhaps the largest and most fruitful there ever was)
and you picked off one bad apple, would you cut
down the entire tree, thus destroying all
the good juicy apples?
Or
Would you simply cast the bad ones down
and gather all the good ones?
~

Can you picture what your life would be like,
if you constantly put others before you?
One thing's for certain, it would be
a pleasing sight to God.
~

Emotions are the result of a choice we make within.

OUT OF IGNORANCE

One of the saddest
things I've discovered with regards to religion,
is that an enormous amount of believer's have
not read their entire book or books pertaining to their
particular faith. Also, they have not made a comparative
study of other religions, so that they may be able
to make an informed or educated decision.

You want to know how *most people* chose their faith?
They don't! They were just simply **born into it.**
Perhaps you are the same religion as your parents?
"Most people" would reply, yes.
But faith is something we are to seek and learn, then
choose, it is not supposed to be something that one is *born
into* like race or sex. How lazy of *a people* are we, to just
accept our religious heritage and not contribute time or
energy to the pursuit truth. Or is it just too difficult
to learn and *be able to discern for oneself?*
Is it ever *wise* to make a decision
(especially one that will determine your eternal life)
OUT OF IGNORANCE?
Or
should they gather as much information as they can,
so to be able to decide for them self?
Now I am in no way insinuating
that one's religion is wrong, based on the sole fact that they
just believed what their parents did.

If you took umbrage to this remark, why do so?
I only stated that it is ignorant,
to choose out of ignorance
and
wise to choose, when educated.

55

Shed yourself of your hypocrisy
by focusing on your own sins, rather than the sins of others.

~

I Love Evolutionist,
I think it's wonderful how God has blessed us all with
freewill, and then gave us the intellectual ability
to choose between GOD and Darwin.

~

The United States is a *predominantly* Christian Nation
that believes in the "freedom of religion".
Because of this, there are numerous religions within the
United States of America
The religion of Islam is free to be practiced in the U.S.A.
yet many of the Muslim nations (those governed in Islam)
not only reject Christians from living in their lands,
they persecute and even at times, kill them.
If you are wondering, could this possibly be true?
Sadly, yes.

~

The moral compass of this world is not broken
it's just that most people don't bother to look at it
and many who do look at it, don't follow it
(The "Word of God" is our compass)

~

The more you give of yourself
the more you are inclined to receive from others.

~

Truth should always be given with
Compassion and Patience
rarely with anger.

Some parents love their kids so much
that they're afraid to discipline them, most of the time it's
because they fear that they won't be loved if they do so.
THIS IS A HUGE MISTAKE
that will likely go undiscovered until the child is grown
and has little to no respect for their parents.
The child will likely do so,
because each time you neglect disciplining a child
for bad behavior, you are promoting that
kind of behavior in your child.
Non-respect or appreciation is often a result of non-
discipline. The word "discipline" often stirs up images of
violence but the word really means is:
Training one to act in accordance with Rules and Respect
If a child often disobeys a parent's rules,
they have *likely* been *trained to do so.*
There's no doubt that being a loving parent is a great
responsibility, for you are the chief molder of a child's
character. The healthiest kind of discipline encourages
understanding between parent and child, and is reinforced
with love. What I mean is, if a child does something bad
make sure you stop them immediately and explain (in a
manner that your child can understand), why it is
that what they're doing is bad and ill behavior
like that will have ill consequences.
Every time your child see's you ignore bad behavior,
they will come to believe that it is acceptable.
Now if your child misbehaves again, **you must** adhere
to your promise and *administer the consequence.*
Consequences can range from time outs, takeaways,
grounded, etc… Results from discipline are (likely) subject
to your child's dislike for that particular consequence, the
more they dislike *the punishment,* the *less likely*
they are to repeat that ill behavior again.
Loving a child is a responsibility.

57

Actions I do that SUPPORT my Faith are...

_____

_____

_____

_____

Actions that OPPOSE my Faith are...

_____

_____

_____

_____

_____

_____

_____

_____

_____

_____

_____

HATE SIN – LOVE SINNERS

I have friends that are Hindu, Catholic, Buddhist, Jewish,
Muslim, Christian, Atheist, Gay, Lesbian, Adulterers,
and even <u>Smoker's.</u>
And I Love them all!!!
If you're wondering *smoker's* is he serious? Yes I am.
In all seriousness they were the hardest for me to
learn to love, I know this may sound ridiculous
to some, but please allow me to try to explain:
<u>Cigarettes are well known to cause cancer, one of the most</u>
<u>deadly diseases known today</u> (you likely know someone
who has died from this horrible disease, as do I). Now if
smoker's are in such a hurry to die, I can not stop them but
I wish they didn't smoke (just as I have found that most
smokers themselves also wish they didn't smoke). What
really gets me the most is that <u>second hand smoke kills,</u>
poisons enter the air and not only pollute my lungs but
everyone else's, children's, baby's, expectant mother's.
Of course,
not everyone who breathes in
second hand smoke will die of cancer
but it has been proven to significantly increase
the risk of cancer. Now if the law can justify killing (<u>if it be</u>
<u>in self defense</u>, *meaning that if someone was trying to kill*
you and you killed them it would be justified), then why is it
not justifiable to kill a smoker and plead self defense?
<u>Of course this is **absolutely absurd** and I am in **NO WAY,**</u>
<u>nor would I ever, promote any one to violence (let alone to</u>
<u>kill another),</u> but I use this crazy "logic" if you will, only to
express my intense **hatred for cigarettes,** notice I said
"cigarettes" and not "smokers" for I stand firm that
I love all smokers. I know it is not God's will
(under any circumstance) that we are to hate
sinner's but we are to hate *sin* only.

59

Before Jesus entered heaven, he told his followers they'd
be persecuted and hated for righteousness sake,
that they would be condemned, beaten, and
possibly even killed, because the world
loves darkness and He is the light.
NO WAY
on Earth does this sound enticing
but Jesus said, "I am Not of this World".
This world loves darkness and hates the light,
so everyone has a decision to make whether they
want to submit to darkness or rise above and shine.

~

ADDICTIONS
Often make one a slave, to that particular sin.
They have empowered the sin so much; that they have
surrendered all control over to it. And once control has
been given up, only that person has the ability to fight
and win it back, but the battle within is the most
difficult to conquer for your adversary knows
all your weakness's and will exploit them
at all costs to maintain that control.
Thus it is wise to seek out an ally, one who can help you
overcome and be victorious. AND WHO could be a greater
ally than GOD? For He knows you even better than you
know yourself. If you equip yourself against the
enemy with a power BEYOND MEASURE
then you are truly ready to overcome.

~

This world is so utterly consumed in darkness that if you're
content in it, you're one self-absorbed person.
Although
if you concern yourself with the well being of others,
then you diminish that darkness with your light.

America:
What would you think if I told you, that every time you put
gas in your car, you are enriching a nation who's sole
religion has a *significant amount* of believers who
view *you* as their <u>enemy</u> and not only do
they hate you, they believe it is
their holy duty to kill you.
This couldn't possibly be true, right?
Wrong.
The people I'm referring to are known as "Islamic radicals"
but understand that a great number of Muslim's
protest that these *terrorists* have distorted
their religion and act out of ignorance.

~

The wicked one has set **HIS** traps,
be wise to **HER** cunningness.

~

When you judge others you condemn only yourself.

~

Those who have hate for others will NEVER
overcome their hatred through violence,
for hatred is a **consuming evil** that will
forever replenish itself with victims.

~

Jesus taught *that if one sins in their mind*
they have sinned in their heart and
thus, is *just as* the one who
has performed the sin.
Therefore,
rebuke sinful thoughts immediately before they
germinate within you and cause you to go astray.

61

The moment a person **FORCES** their religion upon
another, they are acting outside of God's will,
for God granted all of us with "freewill".
Now if God so desired,
He could easily make everyone of us
love Him, but rather than make us,
He allows each of us to choose
whether or not, to love Him.

~

There once was a man, who unknowingly believed in a
"false religion", the devil had enticed the man with lies
and pride, so the man joyfully surrendered his entire
will *to his faith*. The man's only passion was to share
his faith with others, convert them, or kill them.
Nothing could deter this man from his mission,
he was fully dedicated to his *false god*.
Then there was another man, who
believed in the "Truth",
but his faith was lukewarm,
for the devil had entangled him
with fear and doubts, which prevented
him from ever sharing the Truth with others.
Now which man do you think saddened God more?

~

How can a "Christian" know if something is true or not?
They are to simply **look to the Bible**.
If it is true *according to the Bible*, then it is true.
And
If it is not true *according to the Bible*, then it is not true.
Extremely simple, yet frequently not applied.

~

Compliments are an inexpensive way of giving.

Suffering

I have personally experienced tremendous suffering and
sorrow, these experiences have distilled in me a strong
empathy for others who suffer and (as strange as this
may sound) I believe they were also blessings,
because they brought me closer to God.
If you think about it, when do people
think about God the most?
<u>When they are suffering</u>.
This is why we seek God at funerals or when a loved one is
suffering, these hardships are so overwhelming that our
pain causes us to yearn for healing and comforting,
its during these times we seek God the most.
Anything that brings
you *closer to God* is a
Blessing (even suffering).
Does He know your pain? Yes!
Does He know your sorrows? Yes!
Does He want you to come to Him? YES!
Don't wait till you are in agony to want Him.
Need Him now! Think of Him now! Love Him Always!
You will find comfort, if you just put your trust in Him.
Yes, you will continue to have trials and tribulations,
but God will heal your pain and your suffering.
He will bless you until your cup runneth over,
if you just believe.
Love Him and He will never forsake you.
You are more precious to God,
than you can imagine.

~

Even if you lost everyone you would never be alone.

~

I often remember - that I forgot something.

A person may speak to share their beliefs.
But;
A person acts, to show their true beliefs.

"What good is it, my brothers,
if a man claims to have faith but has no deeds?
Can such faith save him?
Suppose a brother or sister is without clothes
and daily food. If one of you says to him,
'Go, I wish you well; keep warm and well fed,'
but does nothing about his physical needs,
what good is it?
In the same way, faith by itself,
if it is not accompanied by action, is dead.
But someone will say,
'You have faith; I have deeds.'
Show me your faith without deeds,
and I will show you my faith by what I do.
You believe that there is one God. Good!
Even the demons believe that—and shudder.
You foolish man,
do you want evidence that faith without deeds is useless?
Was not our ancestor Abraham considered righteous for
what he did when he offered his son Isaac on the altar?
You see that his faith and his actions were working
together, and his faith was made complete by what he did.
And the scripture was fulfilled that says,
"Abraham believed God, and it was credited to him as
righteousness," and he was called God's friend.
You see that a person
is justified by what he does and not by faith alone."
(James 2:14-24)

Accountable
Everyone is subject to *Accountability*.
This means YOU and I, will have
to stand before GOD and explain
(and be responsible for), all of our deeds.
Those who receive much, much will be required
and those who receive little, little will be required.
Desperately seek to forgive those who wrong you,
as you would desire God to forgive you.
And
You by all means love one another,
for love covers a multitude of sins.
Jesus said,
"and I assure you of this: If anyone acknowledges me
*publicly here on earth, **I, the Son of Man,** will openly*
acknowledge that person in the presence of God's angels."
(Luke12:8)
~

If you feel convicted or tormented by your sins
REJOICE
For this is God's way of calling you back to Him.
~

Fear relies upon *lack of faith.*
The more Faith one has, the less they fear.
For if one truly trusts in God, *who* could they possibly fear?
~

One who spends his or her time criticizing others,
is not focusing on how they can improve their self.
~

Look at things the way others do not
and you will see what others do not.

65

Demons in hell,
must constantly get amazed
by how quickly people **BELIEVE**
once they're made to *suffer their consequences.*

~

One of the best ways to show Jesus
HOW MUCH YOU LOVE HIM
is to share that love towards a person
that you like the LEAST.
"...in as much as you have done it
unto one of the least of these my brethren,
you have done it unto me."
(Matthew25:40)

~

Just as a teakettle takes a lot of heat before screaming,
God's **wrath** is building up for all sinners.
Until the day when God removes His **hand of mercy,**
and smites down with great vengeance and furious anger,
all those who opposed His will.
For God declared
VENGEANCE IS MINE
On that great and terrible day many will **cry out to God,**
but God will not hear them, **He will not hear them.**

~

Many people deny God, because "God"
created so much pain and injustice in the world.
When the truth is, God created the world for all of us
to enjoy and take care of, **we added the injustice.**
Being thus, would not their *defiance* then be better placed,
if they denied God for allowing such unworthy,
ungrateful, unholy people (like themselves)
the privilege of living?

66

JUDAISM praises God for **His mercy** yet demands that
you treat neighbors justly, rather than with mercy. For if
someone takes from you it is commanded that you
TAKE IT BACK.
And if someone injures you, **you are to injure
them back** (with equal force). All acts of
unrighteousness are to be returned with
equal debt, so that justice is always
preserved. Indeed in Judaism
God is a God of Righteousness.
CHRISTIANITY praises God for **His mercy** and demands
that you love your enemies and to do good to those
who hurt you. For if someone takes from you,
you are to **GIVE TO THEM.**
If someone asks you to walk a mile, walk two.
In all ways you are to respond with kindness
and **show mercy**. Indeed in Christianity,
God is a God of Righteousness.

~

You've heard it said that,
"People fear what they don't understand".
**THIS IS .
NOT TRUE**
Do you understand "Gravity"?
Do you fully understand "Photosynthesis"?
Do you understand Einstein's "Theory of Relativity"?
Do you even comprehend something as ample as "light"?
There are numerous things in this world, that people
don't understand, yet have absolutely no fear of.
People only fear what they *choose* to fear.

~

One will believe anything another person says,
unless they tell their self differently.

BEWARE of GOOD DEEDS

Good deeds *can* **poison a soul,**
it's venom comes from
Praying, Giving, Fasting, and being Righteous,
because
through acts of goodness,
vanity, pride, and arrogance are often stimulated
and for one to *do good* and think them self above others,
is to become lower than all.
Therefore *good deeds* are only *good* when they abide in
genuine humbleness, only then can it uphold
vanity, pride, and arrogance.

The Parable of the
Pharisee and the Tax Collector
"To some who were confident
of their own righteousness and looked down on
everybody else,
Jesus told this parable:
Two men went up to the temple to pray,
one a Pharisee and the other a tax collector.
The Pharisee stood up and prayed about himself:
'God, I thank you that I am not like other men—robbers,
evildoers, adulterers—or even like this tax
collector. I fast twice a week and
give a tenth of all I get.'
But the tax collector stood at a distance. He would not even
look up to heaven, but beat his breast and said,
'God, have mercy on me, a sinner.'
I tell you that this man, rather than the other,
went home justified before God.
For everyone who exalts himself will be humbled,
and he who humbles himself will be exalted."
(Luke18:9-14)

68

Political System

When someone takes a stance on something,
they are instantly opposed by those who stand for the
opposite. This is why many politicians talk a lot, but say
nothing. For every choice proclaimed creates disapproval
from those who think differently, thus the more they say
the more opposed they become, and in the political
system one progresses much smoother with
the least amount of opposition.
Unfortunately,
this way of thinking promotes
leaders who *stand for* very little.

~

Holding grudges is like throwing a boomerang
they both come back with equal force.

~

If you truly want to feel closer to God,
help a person in dire need.

~

Sin and Salvation

Sin hung on a beautiful tree in the midst of Paradise
and
Salvation hung on a dead tree in a barren hill top.
Coincidence? Perhaps.
But what about when
Adam and Eve were cast out from the Garden of Eden
by God
to a desolate land of <u>thorns</u>, a land tainted by <u>sin</u>.
Could it be mere coincidence then
that the punishment for <u>sin</u> was suffered by a man who was
adorned with nothing but a <u>crown of thorns</u> set upon him
by man?

69

I testify that the following story is true:

Years ago
I was at a used bookstore standing in front of the theology
and philosophy section, there were hundreds of books
I was overwhelmed not knowing which one to read,
so I made a simple prayer in my mind, asking
God to **guide me and direct me** to the
book that *He wanted* me to read.
Then I grabbed a book and opened it, and the very first
thing I saw (written in handwriting inside the cover)
was "Dear Matthew" the message went on to say,
I am so proud of you… Keep up the good work.
Love always (signed by a family member).
What's so strange about this? Well,
my name is *Matthew*. I only
use the name "Elijah"
for my writings.
Now of course I know
the message wasn't intended for me,
but I strongly believe, God used it for me.
I didn't use my real name as author of this book
not because I fear criticism, rejection, or even worse,
but I fear the opposite, compliments, praises, or honor,
because they promote the sense of pride, and I feel if
anyone is touched by my book then only God deserves
the praise (not me). For I am blessed, if my words
have touched your heart, blessed that
God used a sinner like me,
to do His will.
~

Humility is a hard battle to fight,
when *self* is being advertised.

70

My Greatest Achievements in Life have been...

_____

_____

_____

_____

_____

_____

My Greatest Regrets in Life would be...

_____

_____

_____

_____

_____

_____

_____

Beware the Deceivers "compromise"
The Deceiver loves when we compromise "Truth"
because once Truth is compromised,
it is no longer *Truth.*

The Deceiver uses "compromise" as a deceptive ploy,
to turn people away from the word of God, so that
they may lean on their own understanding
(and once you've done that, he's got you).
The Bible says,
"Trust in the LORD with all your heart
and lean not on your own understanding;"
(Proverbs 3:5)
The Deceiver loves to entice people into believing
that "all religions" lead to God.
But Jesus says,
"I am the way and the truth and the life.
No one comes to the Father except through me."
(John 14:6)
The Deceiver loves to entice people into believing
that they should *just live for themselves.*
But Jesus says,
"Whoever finds his life will lose it,
and whoever loses his life for my sake will find it."
(Matthew 10:39)
The Deceiver loves to entice people into believing
that they can live for both God and their self.
But Jesus says,
""No one can serve two masters.
Either he will hate the one and love the other,
or he will be devoted to the one and despise the other..."
(Matthew 6:24)
There is absolutely no compromise in "Truth".
If the Deceiver can't get you to compromise,
he will then try to get you to doubt.

Are *True Things* Truth?

True things are merely those that *seem true*
according to ones opinions and understanding of truth.
But Truth is not a word, it is THE WORD.
And
the devil often chooses to
conceal his lies with *true things*
to make it appear as **Truth**.
For example,
Many people have done horrible atrocities
under the belief, that what they are doing is right.
Such as
Hating, Killing, Casting Judgment,
Excommunicating, Persecuting, Suicide Bombing,
Forsaking, Condemning, Abortion, Child Abuse, Genocide,
and Much, Much More.
How could anyone do this believing they are doing right?
Because according to their
personal opinions and understanding
at the time which they did it
it seemed right for them to do so.
Now if it is right in their mind, but wrong in another's
Who's to say which is correct?
(for they both equally believe *they are right*)
TRUTH SAYS
"Do onto others, as you would have them do to you".
That alone is how one determines
what is right and what is wrong.

People who are wise,
"Treat's others the way they would want to be treated",
because they understand that one day
they to will be measured by how they measured others
thus is the *Wisdom of God.*

73

Would you grasp for something that brought you pain
(like molten hot lava), let alone continue to hold it?
Many people do.
They carry anger in their heart
which makes them bitter, unhappy, and
continuously causes them to suffer.
<u>Anger hurts no one but the
person who carries it.</u>
Let go of your anger.

~

NOT SO LONG AGO,
A father had a child that grew up to be gay
and being that the father considered himself to be a
very "religious man", he disowned his own child.
The child
pleaded and asked his father "Why Father, please…"
the father answered "Because you are a Sinner".
So the child was cast out from home,
and the father never spoke to the child again.
Years later,
the father died and was brought before his
Father (God).
God asked the father "Why did you turn your child away?"
The father replied, "Because he was a sinner"
God then told him
"As you turned away your own child, I now turn you away"
the father pleaded "Why God, please…"
God answered, "Because **YOU** are a Sinner"
So the father was cast out from heaven
and God never spoke to him again.

*"If you do not forgive men their sins,
your Father will not forgive your sins."*
(Matthew 6:15)

74

Religious Scripture is either Truth or it is a Lie

One who only believes 99% of the scripture/s that pertain
to their particular religion, is like one who only believes
1%, for both compromise the integral truth of their faith.
Unfortunately, it is not uncommon
for even Christians to compromise God's word,
to appease their own personal beliefs and/or way of life.
The following lists some examples of such,
When a Christian:
Judges others, denies the miracles of Jesus, believes in
evolution, believes that "Jesus" is not the only way to God,
believes that Jesus was not raised from the dead, believes
that one is justified by their works (rather than through
faith), believes they are to condemn non-Christians,
believes they are righteous in themselves, denies
the deity of Jesus, and the list goes on and on,
but basically, any and all beliefs that
go against **Biblical doctrine**.
The **very instant** anyone alters or rejects even the slightest
bit of *their religions* scripture, they have corrupted their
scripture, because it becomes subjugated to a *countless
barrage of personal opinions*, for even if one "jot"
is tampered with,
there becomes no warrant
to treat the rest of that scripture as "Truth",
other than on the basis of *one's personal opinion*.
Therefore,
adding to, altering, or rejecting any part of scripture,
undermines the very essence of that scripture
and declares it untrue within itself.
Thus,
ones particular religious scripture/s
is either **Truth within itself**
or it is a lie.

75

If a person was **chewing on a big juicy piece of meat**
and
was adamantly claiming themselves to be a **vegetarian**,
would you believe them?
Of course not,
because their actions would
completely contradict their claim.
Yet
many people claim a religion that believes in *one thing*,
then their actions consistently do the exact opposite.

The definition of the word "Religion" is:
the body of persons adhering to
a particular set of beliefs and practices.
But,
God does not desire your pretentious *religion*,
He desires nothing less than ALL OF YOU.

The Parable of the Two Sons
"There was a man who had two sons.
He went to the first and said,
'Son, go and work today in the vineyard.
'I will not,' *he answered,*
*but **later he changed his mind and went.***
Then the father went to the other son
and said the same thing.
*He answered, **'I will, sir,' but he did not go.***
'Which of the two did what his father wanted'?"
(Matthew 21:28-31)
"Not everyone who says to me, 'Lord, Lord,'
will enter the kingdom of heaven,
but only he who does
the will of my Father
who is in heaven."
(Matthew 7:21)

76

INTERESTING FACTS: ABOUT **WIVES** IN RELIGION

JUDAISM
ABRAM (Abraham Patriarch of the human race)
Had one wife and committed **fornication** with his wife's
maidservant "Hagar". Hagar bore Abram an
illegitimate son named "Ishmael".

BUDDHISM
GUATAMA SIDDARTHA (founder of Buddhism)
Had abandoned his wife and son to take on the life
of a wandering ascetic, in search of *enlightenment*.

ISLAM
MUHAMMAD (writer of the Qur'an)
Had **at least 9 wives**, one of which was Aisha, she was 13
years old when her marriage was consummated (according
the body of Islamic law, although *most* Sunni Muslims
claim she was nine when the marriage was consummated).
Although the **Qur'an declares**
men to marry 2, 3, or 4 women (Surah4:3), **the prophet**
Muhammad was allowed as many wives as he desired.
(Surah33:50).
Muhammad had **numerous children.**

MORMONISM
JOSEPH SMITH (founder of the Mormon Church)
Had **30+ wives**, many of which were **teenagers** and at
least **eleven of them, were already legally married**
with husbands at the time of their "sealing".
He had numerous children.

CHRISTIANITY
JESUS (son of the Virgin Mary)
Had no wife, nor any children.

What does it mean to JUDGE NOT?
SURELY
if someone is sinning
you are to *discern* (recognize) that they are sinning,
but the problem arises when people mistake
discerning sin* with that of *judging a sinner.
LISTEN
if someone is doing evil and you say "They are **doing** evil"
then you have **Discerned Justly**
and they could be subject to fair punishment.
But
if someone is doing evil and you say "They **are** evil"
you have not discerned,
you have casted **Unjust Judgment.**
For it is NOT JUST
that a sinner be *judged*
BY ANOTHER SINNER.
Judgment belongs to ONE only!
One who is without sin, thus worthy to Judge.
AGAIN
it is **right to discern sin**
and prescribe adequate punishment,
but it is not right to cast judgment upon another
when they themselves are also *transgressors of the law.*

"Brothers, do not slander one another.
Anyone who speaks against his brother or judges him
speaks against the law and judges it. When you judge the
law, you are not keeping it, but sitting in judgment on it.
There is only one Lawgiver and Judge,
the one who is able to save and destroy.
But you—who are you to judge your neighbor?"
(James4:11-12)

"JUDGE NOT OR YE BE JUDGED"

78

UNBELIEVABLE
But true:
In the month of
October, 1536, a man
by the name of William Tyndale,
was tortured and punished to death.
According to the Roman Catholic Church,
William Tyndale was a **"heretic"** for he had committed
an atrocity against the Church, one **punishable by death.**
William was attempting to translate the Bible *into English*.
YES
just in case you missed it
"translating the Bible into English".
William Tyndale a devout servant of God
believed full heartedly that the *Word of God*
should be accessible to anyone who wanted to read it.
This belief, caused the Roman Church to condemn William
as a heretic, they sentenced him to be burned at the stake,
but just before he perished he shouted his last words...
"Lord, open the King of England's eyes"
The Lord must have heard his prayer,
because one year after the slain
of William Tyndale,
a man by the name of John Rodgers (who had worked with
William), was hired by the King of England, to create an
English version of the Bible, that became known as
the King James version.
Shortly after the vicious murder of William Tyndale,
his work became admired, by the very organization
that persecuted, tortured, and killed him.

Today,
almost every
Catholic Church in the world
contains a Bible written in *English*.

THE BIBLE OR *TRADITIONS OF MEN*
Interesting scripture,
with regards to
teachings and traditions of men;

"They worship me in vain;
their teachings are but rules taught by men.
You have let go of the commands of God and
*are holding on to the **traditions of men**."*
(Mark7:7-8, Matthew15:9)

"Thus you nullify the word of God
*by **your tradition** that you have handed down..."*
(Mark7:13)

"See to it that no one takes you captive
through hollow and deceptive philosophy,
*which depends on **human tradition** and*
the basic principles of this world
rather than on Christ."
(Colossians 2:8)

*"Woe to you, **teachers of the law** and Pharisees,*
you hypocrites! You clean the outside of the cup and dish,
but inside they are full of greed and self-indulgence."
(Matthew 23:25)

Interesting fact:
Protestant Christianity is *Biblically Based*
It claims *itself* dependant upon none
other than the Word of God.
And
Catholicism is *Church Based*
It claims within *itself* to be dependant upon
The Pope and *Traditions/Teachings* of Men

80

**Both Judaism and Christianity celebrate
"Passover" and "The Feast of Unleavened Bread"**
Remember
that the "roots" of Christianity are found within Judaism,
only Christians believe that Jesus was the fulfillment of
prophecy regarding the coming of the Messiah.
Now leaven is a substance
which causes fermentation and expansion of dough.
The Feast of Unleavened Bread, celebrates *Passover*, the
day God brought His people out of the bonds of Egypt.
God says,
""This is a day you are to commemorate; for the
generations to come you shall celebrate it as a festival to
the LORD -a lasting ordinance. For seven days you are to
eat bread made without yeast. On the first day remove
the yeast from your houses, for whoever eats anything
with yeast in it from the first day through the seventh
must be cut off from Israel. On the first day hold a
sacred assembly, and another one on the seventh day.
Do no work at all on these days, except to prepare
food for everyone to eat—that is all you may do."
(Exodus12:14-16)
Why is *unleavened bread* so important?
besides the fact, that the word appears 30 times in the Bible
To understand why,
one must first understand how *leaven* works,
the slightest amount of leaven can corrupt the whole,
for leaven infests amounts many times greater than itself.
Leaven is symbolic for **sin**, how even the smallest sin can
corrupt the entire body. The Jews were instructed to
destroy all the leaven in the house by burning it.
PASSOVER
Is the day of Unleavened Bread
on which the ***Passover lamb*** had to be sacrificed.
God used

81

Unleavened Bread to signify the *Community of Israel*
and
The Blood of a Lamb, to save *His people.*

Years later,
*"It was just before the Passover Feast. Jesus knew that the
time had come for him to leave this world and go to the
Father. Having loved his own who were in the world,
he now showed them the full extent of his love."*
(John13:1)
And during this Passover meal
Jesus partook on his
Last Supper.
He took **unleavened bread,**
gave thanks and **broke it**
saying to his disciples,
"This is my body given for you;
do this in remembrance of me."
In the same manner,
he took the cup and said,
"This cup is the **new covenant in my blood,**
which is poured out for you.

Now when Jesus broke the Unleavened Bread,
**He was breaking the old community of Israel and
establishing a new community,** one free from the limits
of heritage, one that would accept **both Jews and Gentiles.**
The Bible says,
*"Is God the God of Jews only?
Is he not the God of Gentiles too? Yes, of Gentiles too,
since there is only one God, who will justify the
circumcised by faith and the uncircumcised through that
same faith. Do we, then, nullify the law by this faith?
Not at all! Rather, we uphold the law."*
(Roman3:29-31)

And when Jesus declared a new covenant,
He was declaring that
"But now a **righteousness** *from God, apart from law,*
has been made known,
to which the Law and the Prophets testify.
This righteousness from God **comes through**
faith in Jesus Christ to all who believe.
There is no difference, for all have sinned and fallen short
of the glory of God, and are justified freely by his grace
through the redemption that came by Christ Jesus.
God presented him as a sacrifice of atonement, through
faith in his blood. He did this to demonstrate his justice,
because in his forbearance he had left the sins committed
beforehand unpunished—he did it to demonstrate his
justice at the present time, so as to be just and the
one who justifies those who have faith in Jesus. "
(Roman3:21-26)

"For what the law was powerless to do
in that it was weakened by the sinful nature,
God did by sending his own Son in the likeness of
sinful man to be a sin offering.
And so he condemned sin in sinful man, in order that the
righteous requirements of the law might be fully met in us,
who do not live according to the sinful nature
but according to the Spirit. "
(Romans8:3-4)

Jesus told his followers
"A new command I give you: Love one another.
As I have loved you, so you must love one another.
By this all men
will know that you are my disciples,
if you love one another. "
(John13:34-35)

How Could a Loving God do This?

There once was a couple, who couldn't bear children, they couldn't understand how a loving God would let so many other couples be able to have babies *but not them.*

There once was a woman, who was very sad and alone, she couldn't understand how a loving God would let so many other women find a man and get married *but not her.*

There once was a man, who was going through a divorce, he couldn't understand how a loving God would let so many other men live happily married lives *but not him.*

There once was a parent, who lost a child at a young age, the parent couldn't understand how a loving God would let so many other children grow up *but not hers.*

There once was a girl, who lost the use of her legs in a car accident, she couldn't understand how a loving God would let so many other girls are able to run and play *but not her.*

There once was a young man, who was dying from a deadly disease, he couldn't understand how a loving God would let other people live long healthy lives *but not him.*

There once was a family, who lost their home and all of their possessions in a fire. They just didn't understand "How could a loving God do this *to them?*"

ASK YOURSELF,
are you thankful for everything God has given you
or
are you waiting to blame God *and resent Him*
the moment He takes something away?

84

God vs. Atheism:

If you were to look at God mathematically
and use nothing but sound judgment
one could only ascertain two possibilities either
THERE *IS* A GOD
or
THERE *IS NOT* A GOD.

Under the premise that there is "No God"
When an atheist dies,
nothing happens, absolutely **nothing.**
And
when a believer dies,
nothing happens, absolutely **nothing.**
NOW
Under the premise that there "Is a God"
when an atheist dies,
they are **tormented and suffer for an eternity**
and
when a believer dies,
they **enter heaven and live forever with God.**
SO
from a **strictly logical standpoint** only a person who
completely lacks any kind of common sense *whatsoever*
could prescribe to the belief that
there is no God.
Now from
a *statistical point of view* it would be less ignorant
for a person to **reject a FREE lottery ticket**
(one with a 50/50 probability of winning MILLIONS)
than it would be for a person to reject God.
Because logically speaking
an atheist obtains *Nothing or Eternal Suffering*
and a believer obtains *Nothing or Eternal Happiness.*
Therefore, atheism completely lacks intelligence.

85

Christian Leaders

There's a lot of Christian Leaders in the world today
and many of which, disagree with one another.
Therefore be wise and take the initiative.
Read the Bible and uncover the Truth for yourself.

"Dear friends, do not believe every spirit, but test
the spirits to see whether they are from God,
because many false prophets have
gone out into the world."
(1 John 4:1)

Unfortunately there are even "Christian Leaders" today
that preach messages that are not Biblically based.
One example
of this is when a preacher "claims" to
know when of the end of the world will come.
They say this despite that fact that the Bible says,
"No one knows about that day or hour, not
even the angels in heaven, nor the Son,
but only the Father".
(Matthew 24:36 and Mark 13:32)

Truth within the Christian faith comes from abiding
within the Bible (Read Isaiah 42:9), we are to test all things
to the Word of God and hold fast to that which is good.
So if a "Christian Leader" is professing a message that
opposes scripture, we can either choose to believe
that they have more wisdom than God, or we can
rebuke (correct) them with kindness and patience.

"FAITH should not be in the wisdom of men,
but in the POWER OF GOD"
(1 Corinthians 2:5).

86

What is Right? - What is Wrong?
This question has confounded
some of the most intellectual minds of all time,
ironically the answer is elementary.
If you
Love your neighbor as yourself
you are doing right.
If you
Don't Love your neighbor as yourself
you are doing wrong.
Only through the act of
"Treating others the way you would want to be treated"
does one understand right from wrong.
~

Jesus never said, come to **Christianity**
Jesus never said, come to a **System**
Jesus never said, come to **Religion**
Jesus simply said, **"Come, Follow Me"**
~

POLITICS
It is not uncommon for politics to be about
Wheeling and Dealing,
rather than addressing the common good of it's citizens.
This happens simply because of you,
YOU LET IT HAPPEN.
Sadly the *common person* doesn't care about issues
that don't affect them directly. In other words,
only if it disturbs "Their Way of Life",
DO THEY CARE
yet as soon as *Their Way of Life* is disturbed
they expect (and sometimes demand) everyone else to care.
Politics are often a reflection of
Social Negligence.

Judaism strictly believes "God is one"

This perhaps *more than any other piece of scripture,* is the primary reason why believers in Judaism, don't believe that Jesus was the messiah (pronounced by the prophets). For Jesus equated himself with God, saying, "I and the Father are one". But anyone who equates them self (or anyone for that matter), with God, is committing one Judaism's greatest sins "polytheism".

Yet in Genesis 1:26, according to Judaic scripture (just before God is about to make the first man "Adam") God spoke,

"Let us make man in our image, after our likeness".

US and OUR

Are both irrevocably plural.

So why then did God speak with regards to Himself as deliberately non-singular?

Who could God possibly be referring to, when He says "our likeness"? **Who** is like unto God? **Who** does God equate Himself with, when He says **"our likeness"**?

To speak such words, could only constitute that there is another, who is "like God".

Many Christians believe this is the first evidential statement regarding "God the Father" and "God the Son".

Another instance, found in the Book of Psalms chapter 110:1, it reads " *The LORD saith unto my lord:*

'Sit thou at My right hand, until I make thine enemies thy footstool'."

Here again we see the words are specific and deliberate, "The LORD", who hardly anyone can contest is **God**, so in other words, "Then '**God'**, said to 'my Lord'…"

Now **who** is God speaking to in this passage?

Who is "my Lord"?

Once again Christians believe this is evidential support to "God the Father" and "God the Son".

The most "ignorant" question ever asked

"How could God let bad things happen to *good* people?"
The sheer
Ignorance of this Question
could only be surpassed by asking it twice.

Non-believers often ask this question, not to be answered,
but rather to pompously display their intellect and mock
God in the process. On the other hand, there are some,
who ask this question sincerely, and it is for them,
that I will resolve to answer this question. First,
one must *truly want to know the answer*, this
may sound simple, **Truth** is **easily desired,**
but what people fail to comprehend is that
TRUTH is extremely difficult to face.
Therefore if you are willing, to hear me,
HEAR ME;
None of us are GOOD, no, not even one!!!
We are ALL sinners. We are ALL unrighteous.
WE ARE ALL
defilers, transgressors, unjust, wretched, filthy, unworthy,
AND COMPLETELY **UNCLEAN** BEFORE THE LORD.
God's *Holiness* is so pure that even the
slightest sin is an abomination to Him.
No matter if you have committed one sin or a million sins,
YOU ARE GUILTY.
Now one may say, "Yes, I am a sinner, but I'm not as guilty
as another", none the less **you are a TRANGRESSOR!!!**
And God is a RIGHTEOUS God, A JUST God,
A Holy, Holy, Holy, God.
For God NOT to punish sin or just ignore sin
would make Him
UNJUST, UNRIGHTEOUS, AND UNHOLY.
Therefore, God MUST ABSOLUTELY punish sin.

89

Now

"Has God ever let bad things happen to good *people*?"

NO

"Has God ever let bad things happen to a good person?"

YES

In fact,

God allowed

horrible atrocities

happen to a good person.

*(Remember, no one is **good**, except for God)*

THE ONLY TIME

God ever permitted bad things to happen to a good person

was in **Jesus Christ.**

God served His Judgment on *sin*,

He directed ALL of His Anger, All of His Wrath

(THAT WAS DUE TO ALL OF US SINNERS)

and placed it on His only begotten son

JESUS.

Not only did Jesus *lay down his own life for us,* he bore our
sins, the sins of the whole world, so that God could redeem
us, through him. He took every bit of God's righteous anger
towards sin, all the hatred, all the condemnation, all the
persecution, the mockeries, the insults, every whip
and scorn. He took upon himself everything
that was rightfully due to us

SINNERS

so that we *may* be saved by grace.

To wonder

"How could God let bad things happen to *good* people?"

Oh ye of little faith and understanding, you should ask,

"How could God let good things happen to you, a sinner?"

We have been given SO MUCH of God's mercy that the
moment He takes away His *grace,* we get angry.

This wicked generation, should ask themselves

"Why does God love us so much?"

TWO ACCOUNTS OF PROPHECY:
Regarding the coming Messiah
Found in the Jewish Bible
The first account found in:
Neviim - The Prophets
Yisheyah – (Isaiah 53:3-12)

3

He was despised, and forsaken of men, a man of pains,
and acquainted with disease, and as one from
whom men hide their face: he was despised,
and we esteemed him not.

4

Surely our diseases he did bear, and our pains he carried;
whereas we did esteem him stricken,
smitten of God, and afflicted.

5

But he was wounded because of our transgressions,
he was crushed because of our iniquities:
the chastisement of our welfare was upon him,
and with his stripes we were healed.

6

All we like sheep did go astray, we turned every one to his
own way; and LORD hath
made to light on him the iniquity of us all.

7

He was oppressed, though he humbled himself and opened
not his mouth; as a lamb that is led to the slaughter, and
as a sheep that before her shearers is dumb; yea,
he opened not his mouth.

8

By oppression and judgment he was taken away, and with
his generation who did reason? For he was cut off out of
the land of the living, for the transgression of my people
to whom the stroke was due.

9

And they made his grave with the wicked, and with the rich
his tomb; although he had done no violence, neither was
any deceit in his mouth.'
10
Yet it pleased LORD to crush him by disease; to see if his
soul would offer itself in restitution, that he might see his
seed, prolong his days, and that the purpose of LORD
might prosper by his hand:
11
Of the travail of his soul he shall see to the full, even My
servant, who by his knowledge did justify the Righteous
One to the many, and their iniquities he did bear.
12
Therefore will I divide him a portion among the great, and
he shall divide the spoil with the mighty; because he
bared his soul unto death, and was numbered with
the transgressors; yet he bore the sin of many,
and made intercession for the transgressors.

All of the above is found in just ONE small section of the
Jewish Bible, located in THE PROPHETS.
The Second account is found in:
Ketuvim - The Writings
Tehilim – (Psalms 118:21-22)
21
"I will give thanks unto Thee, for Thou hast answered me,
and art **become my salvation**.
22
**The stone which the builders rejected
is become the chief corner-stone.**"

I find this to be one of the most profound prophecies in
scripture, because it states that the savior (who is to become
salvation) is destined to be rejected by the religious
authorities in Judaism "the builders".

92

And furthermore,
that this "rejected stone"
is to become "the chief corner-stone".
*Definition of corner-stone: the chief foundation
on which something is constructed or developed.*
Within this prophecy one could only acknowledge
that **if the Jewish leaders didn't reject Jesus**, then he
would not fulfill this prophecy, and then in no way could
he possibly be the *salvation* (spoken of in scripture).
But by *rejecting him* they solidify this prophecy
and add to the already substantial amounts
of evidence that affirm Jesus truly is
THE MESSIAH.

Please remember,
these are only *two portions* of Judaic prophecy
found in **The Tanakh** (the Jewish Bible),
among MANY, MANY PROPHECIES.

I'm aware
that people are often stubborn, and that
they'll believe *only what they choose to believe* ,
rather than base their decision on the basis of evidence,
and that no amount of contradictory evidence
within their own religious text, could
ever persuade them differently.
Because
Jesus himself said,
*"How foolish you are, and how slow of heart to believe all
that the prophets have spoken! Did not the Christ have
to* **suffer these things and then enter his glory?**
*And beginning with Moses and all the Prophets,
he explained to them what was said in all
the Scriptures concerning himself."*
(Luke 24:25-27)

93

Jesus told his people,
"You diligently study the Scriptures
because you think that by them you possess eternal life.
These are the Scriptures that testify about me,
yet you refuse to come to me to have life.
I do not accept praise from men, but I know you.
I know that you do not have the love of God in your hearts.
I have come in my Father's name, and you do not accept
me; but if someone else comes in his own name, you will
accept him. How can you believe if you accept praise
from one another, yet make no effort to obtain
the praise that comes from the only God?
But do not think I will accuse you before the Father.
Your accuser is Moses, *on whom your hopes are set.*
If you believed Moses, you would believe me, for he wrote
about me. But since you do not believe what he wrote,
how are you going to believe what I say?"
(John 5:39-47)
"O Jerusalem, Jerusalem, you who kill the prophets and
stone those sent to you, how often I have longed to gather
your children together, as a hen gathers her chicks
under her wings, but you were not willing."
(Matthew 23:37 and Luke 13:34)
"Whoever believes and is baptized will be saved,
but whoever does not believe will be condemned."
(Mark 16:16)
"I tell you that one greater than the temple is here. If you
*had known what these words mean, '**I desire mercy, not***
***sacrifice,**' you would not have condemned the innocent."*
(Matthew 12:6-7)
"If anyone is ashamed of me and my words
in this adulterous and sinful generation, the Son of Man
will be ashamed of him when he comes in
his Father's glory with the holy angels."
(Mark 8:38)

94

"True Believers" in Christ
The Lord says...
"When I bring the sword against a land,
and the people of the land choose one of their men and
make him their watchman, and he sees the sword coming
against the land and blows the trumpet to warn the people,
then if anyone hears the trumpet but does not take warning
and the sword comes and takes his life, his blood will be on
his own head. Since he heard the sound of the trumpet but
did not take warning, his blood will be on his own head.
If he had taken warning, he would have saved himself.
But if the watchman
sees the sword coming and does not blow the trumpet
to warn the people and the sword comes and takes
the life of one of them, that man will be taken
away because of his sin, but I will hold the
watchman accountable for his blood. "
(Ezekiel 33:1-6)
The Day of the Lord is coming,
and my horn is blowing!!!
Believers, we are the watchmen, if we do not
sound the alarm and preach the Word of God
(so that the non-believers may be able to believe),
then "we" will be held accountable for their blood.
God commands that we "GO" and preach the gospel.
(2 Corinthians 5:20; Mark 16:15; Romans 10:14-17;
Jeremiah 1:7-10,17, 20:9; Acts 1:8, 20:26-27; Luke 19:10;
Ephesians 4:14-15; 2 Timothy 2:2, 4:1-5; Isaiah 55:11;
Matthew 28:19-20, John 10:11, 16; 20:21)
"...Faith comes from hearing the message,
and the message is heard through the word of Christ."
I lose sleep in anguish that I am not able to warn everyone.
I weep for all of those who deny God's gift of salvation.
I ache for them. I pray for them. I tremble for them.
I wrote this book for them.

Opinions and Scripture

What one believes about one's religion is irrelevant,
**if it does not stand firm in accordance to the doctrine
or doctrines that pertain to that specific religion.**
For instance,
I once heard a man say,
"I'm Catholic, but I don't believe in the Pope"
this would be like a Christian saying,
"I'm Christian, but I don't believe in Jesus"
or for a Muslim to say, "I believe in the Koran,
but not in Allah". **To do such, would completely
contradict the definition of what it means *to be such.***
Therefore, it is important to understand that relevance,
or "validity" is only gained, when beliefs uphold to the
particular religions doctrines. This is very important
because otherwise utter chaos and non-sense
would run the gamut, and personal "opinions"
would be just as equal to scripture itself.
As you may no doubt know, human beings have a strong
tendency to change things around them, to accommodate
their self (and religion is no different). You will find
that it is not unusual for believers to take what they
agree with (from their religion of choice), then
alter or disregard the rest, just as if they were
taking out pickles from a cheeseburger.
After all if one's going to take a bite
why not make it fit their tastes,
RIGHT?
But religion is not like a cheeseburger,
one can't simply pull things out or add things to it, in order
to accommodate their particular "tastes", because beliefs
that oppose text **"by definition"** (in accordance to that
religion), are fabricated falsehoods that defile the
truth and integrity of that specific religion.
Therefore,

96

"religious truth", is only ascertained and proven through **scriptural support**, which pertains to that given religion. For instance,
One is a Buddhist, inasmuch as one adheres to
the teachings the Buddha.
One is a Muslim, inasmuch as one adheres to
the Koran (also spelled Qur'an).
One is a Catholic, inasmuch as one adheres to
the Roman Catholic Church.
One is a Christian, inasmuch as one adheres to
the *teachings of Jesus.*
And so on.

If you're curious as to why I didn't put the "teachings of Jesus" for the Roman Catholic Church, it's simply because the Catholic Church is a **hierarchy.**
Hierarchy is a governing system where persons rank one above another.
According to Catholic doctrine, a Catholics primary allegiance is to be to the "Church" first and then the Bible (which conveys the teachings of Jesus). "The Church" claims this because they believe that the Bible could possibly be "misinterpreted", thus hindering one's possibility for salvation. And being that the Catholic Church **"claims to be infallible"** *(perfect, without flaw, and incapable of error), they then "never" misinterpret scripture, and this is why all "true Catholics" are first and foremost called upon to adhere to* the **Roman Catholic Church.**

~

Fears greatest power *lies* in thee illusion of itself.

~

Pride is a slayer to the self-righteous.

The problem with "self-help" books, is
that they all *tend* to focus on the wrong person.
"SELF",
by definition *is a selfish word.*
No matter what anyone may achieve in this world
whether it be fame, fortune, power, and/or all sorts
of earthly pleasures, these will all come to pass,
but the
SOUL REMAINS FOREVER.
For what does it profit a man
if he gains the whole world but loses his own soul?
The only way to truly live a rich and meaningful life,
is through the *selfless* act of **helping others.**
Jesus said *"lose your life for my sake,*
and you will find it".
~

If
I were
to tell you that
"I Love Sinners",
when you read "Sinners" who comes to your mind?
Murderers. Rapists. Thieves. Maybe you think of
Adulterers, or perhaps Homosexuals. Everyone
has there own unique perspective of what
a sinner is, but the only perspective
that even means anything is **God's.**
And according to God's perspective,
everyone alive today is a sinner. Not one
of us **is without sin, for we have all sinned.**
So when I say, "I love sinners" it simply means
I LOVE YOU.
I LOVE
YOU
All

Hypocrites in Christianity

Hypocrisy is not a slander to the Christian faith,
but on the contrary, it is a testimony to the Truth of Jesus.
For Jesus himself said,
*"...these people honor me with their lips,
but their hearts are far from me."*
(Mark 7:6)
*"Watch out for false prophets. They come to you in sheep's
clothing, but inwardly they are ferocious wolves...
Thus, by their fruit you will recognize them."*
(Matthew 7:15-20)

~

There's far less "evidential support"
for the *Theory of Evolution*, than there is for *Jesus*.
Yet some people have no problem at all,
claiming evolution as "fact".
Evolution is being referenced as:
the ability of random mutation and natural selection,
accounting for the complexity of life.
For more information on the flaws in evolution,
I suggest reading "Fatal Flaws" by Hank Hanegraaff.

~

God gives to us freely, and only commands in return
that we give *a tenth* (of what He gave us) to help the needy.
Yet most of us ignore God's word and chose to waste our
money on personal desires and passing pleasures.
For more information on giving to the needy,
I suggest saving a life by sponsoring
a child at www.worldvision.com

~

The wise focus their attention on sharing the Truth
while the unwise set out to condemn lies.

The Koran proclaims
that Jesus did not die on the cross,
but that *a look alike* was killed in his place.
Yet not only biblical evidence, but also historical
evidence supports that Jesus *did die on the cross.*
For more information, I suggest reading
"The Case for the Real Jesus"
by Lee Strobel.

~

Strive to be last (by humbling yourself before others),
so that God may regard you as first.

~

The wise seek to please God
whereas the unwise seek to please men.
"Do not conform any longer to the pattern of this world,
but be transformed by the renewing of your mind.
Then you will be able to test and approve what
God's will is—his good, pleasing and perfect will."
For more information on becoming transformed,
I suggest reading "Renewing Your Mind" by R.C. Sproul

~

You were created for one reason,
FOR THE PLEASURE OF GOD.
You are not an accident, you were made *absolutely unique*
and for the purpose of knowing God, so that you
may have a relationship with Him.
For more information on *the meaning of life,*
I suggest reading "Purpose Driven Life" by Rick Warren.

~

Seek not to praise yourself,
but constantly compliment others.

100

**How cunning is the Deceiver that he has
beguiled the whole world.**

Many people believe that God rewards the faithful
through material gifts, not realizing that it is Satan
who tantalizes *us* with his materials (in hopes to
turn us away from God, by increasing our
appetite for the things of this world).
**If we are focused on OUR WANTS,
it becomes easy to overlook what God desires.**

"For where our treasure is, there your heart will be also."
(Matthew 6:21 and Luke 12:34)

Some people claim that since *they are children of God*,
God then will graciously bestow His favors upon them
in the forms of material wealth.
Such as a big house, an expensive car, and lots of money,
all the things that this world so craves and loves.
Yet Truth is,
it gives the Deceiver great pleasure
when we lust for things of this (material) world.

*"Do not love the world or anything in the world.
If anyone loves the world,
the love of the Father is not in him.
For everything in the world—the cravings of sinful man,
the lust of his eyes and the boasting of what he has and
does—comes not from the Father but from the world.
The world and its desires pass away, but the man
who does the will of God lives forever."*
(1 John 2:15-17)

The Bible tells us:
"No one can serve two masters. Either he will hate the one

and love the other, or he will be devoted to the one and despise the other. <u>You cannot serve both God and Money</u>."
(Matthew 6:24 and Luke 16:13)

"Blessed are the meek, for they will inherit the earth."
(Matthew 5:5)

"It is easier for a camel to go through the eye of a needle than for a rich man to enter the kingdom of God."
(Matthew 19:24, Mark 10:25, and Luke 18:25)

"For the love of money is a root of all kinds of evil. Some people, eager for money, have wandered from the faith and pierced themselves with many grief's."
(1 Timothy 6:10)

"Keep your lives free from the love of money and be content with what you have, because God has said, 'Never will I leave you; never will I forsake you'."
(Hebrews 13:5)

"Has not my hand made all these things, and so they came into being?" declares the LORD. "This is the one I esteem: he who is humble and contrite in spirit, and trembles at my word."
(Isaiah 66:2)

"For whoever exalts himself will be humbled and whoever humbles himself will be exalted."
(Matthew 23:12, Luke 14:11, Luke 18:14)

... "God opposes the proud but gives grace to the humble. Humble yourselves, therefore, under God's mighty hand, that he may lift you up in due time."
(1 Peter 5:5-6)

The Book of Revelation

Proclaims a great and dreadful day, when God will bring
His Judgment and Wrath upon the whole world.

You may ask yourself:
How could a loving, merciful God,
do such a thing?
But I ask you,
is it not "Just" that sin be punished?
Is it not "Right" for God to punish the wicked?
"For Vengeance is Mine", say's the LORD.

"This is how it will be at the end of the age
The angels will come and separate the wicked from
the righteous and throw them into the fiery furnace,
where there will be weeping and gnashing of teeth."
(Matthew 13:49-50)

We must understand that
"today", is a day of God's Mercy, only by
His Grace, have we been offered Redemption.
It is only because of His amazing love for us, that He is
patient with us sinners (so that we may turn away from our
transgressions and accept that Jesus paid the **"entire price"**
for our sins). For the day of God's Judgment will appear
like a thief in the night and the time of mercy will pass
away. We have been warned by the power of
God's Word
that "the punishment for sin is death".
And in God's Word, Jesus tells us,
"I am the resurrection and the life.
He who believes in me will live, even though he dies;
and whoever lives and believes in me will never die."
(Found in John 11:25-26)

The following contains a brief overview of various religions.

Please keep in mind that all religions have some level of disagreements amongst believers, and that this is just a synopsis or general depiction of that faith.

The religion of Buddhism believes:

Only through *ignorance* do people indulge in the dream
that they are separate, self-existent entities and that *self*
is but an error, for it is the *illusion of self* which causes
all pain, suffering, and sorrow. For life, through the
clinging of *self* is perpetual suffering and dying
(through never ending reincarnation). And
only through **Enlightenment** does one
obtain **Nirvana** which is the bliss of truth
and the end of suffering. The self-indulgent are
slaves to their own passions, but those in whom *self*
has become extinct, are freed from desire; for they desire
neither worldly, nor heavenly pleasures. And their natural
wants defile them not, as long as it be under moderation,
eat and drink according to the needs of the body.

This is **The Middle Path,**
Explained in the Buddha's teachings through
the *Four Noble Truths.*
The Noble Truth of Suffering, that life is filled with
suffering from birth, to death.
The Noble Truth of the Cause of Suffering, found in the
desires of worldly illusions.
The Noble Truth of Cessation of Suffering, remove desire
which lies at the root of all human suffering, then thirst will
die out and suffering will cease.
The fourth Noble Truth is the Path to the Cessation of
Suffering, known as the
Noble Eightfold Path
This path consists of:
Right-view, right-thought, right speech, right-behavior,
right livelihood, right-effort, right mindfulness,
right-concentration.

This *Noble Eightfold Path* is believed to open eyes
and bestow understanding which leads to higher
wisdom, to full enlightenment, to Nirvana.
To lose ones "self"
They must simply become aware, that there is no "self" in
which for them to lose (only the craving of 'self' gives it
existence), only by understanding, that others, are the same
as you, you will come to understand, that while there is
death in "self", there is immortality in this truth. Through
the practice, that all things are made of one essence (yet
they are different according to the forms, which they
assume, for as they form themselves, they so act,
and as they act, so they are), then you will gain
"Enlightenment" which is the path of the Buddha.
"Buddha"
simply means "a fully enlightened one"
who has put an end to the perpetual cycle of rebirth,
by shedding disillusions of self, and living in accord to the
"Dharma".
They believe every living being has the potential
to become a Buddha, and reach enlightenment.
They believe everyone is subject to Karma
(the law of cause and effect).
That the present life reaps what the past has sown,
and the future is determined upon the present.
Those who do good, receive good karma,
thus are rewarded, those who have
done wicked, receive bad karma
and will be tormented.
Buddhism does not believe in God, because that which is
absolute cannot be a cause. That it is neither self, nor
causeless chance, which creates us, but rather "deeds",
which produce both good and bad merit. So, believers are
inclined to **abandon the heresy of worshipping God and
of praying to him**, because they do nothing, nor rituals,

nor fasting, nor going naked, nor shaving the head, nor
sacrificing animals. But only by abandoning desire
and lust, does one become free from evil. A
believer is to purify the heart and mind,
and focus on doing good, so that
good results from their deeds.
In Buddhism, **"one must be a lamp onto there self."**

Some people associate Buddhism with that of a fat Chinese
man, who is always sitting and smiling (generally referred
to as the happy Buddha), ironically Buddhism began with a
very thin prince born in northern India, his name was
Siddhãrtha Gautama. Siddhãrtha gave up all the luxuries of
royalty, to pursue a life of an ascetic, he practiced extreme
self-denial and self-mortification for the pursuit of
"the end of suffering".
He practice meditation, and it was during one meditation,
that he overheard two people passing by on a small boat,
one of them had a string instrument and was explaining to
the other, that the strings cannot be to loose or to tight,
Siddhãrtha opened his eyes to this wisdom and thus was
born the "middle path". He began to share his teachings
with other men, denying that women were worthy (for he
believed they would be the end of Buddhism), and it was
only by the constant requests from Buddha's cousin
Ananda, that he allowed women to partake in his teachings.

All the Buddha's teachings were written by his disciples,
onto palm leaves, in Pali and Sanskrit, ancient Indian
languages, these books are called Sutras and the collection
of these Sutras are know as "Tripitaka" or *Three baskets*.
Many Buddhist celebrate *Buddha Day*
On this day, believers take part in the ceremonial bathing
of the Buddha. They pour water and flowers over
a statue of a baby Siddhartha.

Some quotes of the Buddha

"Do not dwell in the past, do not dream of the future,
concentrate the mind on the present moment."

"All that we are is the result of what we have thought. If a
man speaks or acts with an evil thought, pain follows him.
If a man speaks or acts with a pure thought, happiness
follows him, like a shadow that never leaves him."

"Every human being
is the author of his own health or disease."

"He who loves 50 people has 50 woes;
he who loves no one has no woes."

"No one saves us but ourselves. No one can and
no one may. We ourselves must walk the path."

"Work out your own salvation. Do not depend on others."

"The whole secret of existence is to have no fear.
Never fear what will become of you, depend on no one.
Only the moment you reject all help are you freed."

"Peace comes from within. Do not seek it without."

The founder of Buddhism
the original Buddha, often declared
that women lacked the capacity to understand
and practice the teachings of non-attachment to self,
he believed women were mentally inferior to men.
One of Buddha's quotes on women,
"It is nature's law that rivers wind, trees grow wood, and,
given the opportunity, women work iniquity."

My Personal Views on Buddhism are:

_____

_____

_____

_____

_____

_____

_____

_____

_____

_____

_____

_____

_____

_____

The religion of Christianity believes:

This religion is founded upon salvation, through faith in God's only son Jesus, and only by believing in Him, can one be "saved". They believe God is one, represented as the Father, the Son, and the Holy Spirit.

Christians believe in the Bible.
Which contains
the "Old Testament" and the "New Testament".
The Old Testament contains the sacred writings of the Jews
it consists of God's Law, His Covenants with His people,
History, and Prophecy of a coming Messiah,
who is to be the Savior to His people
and bring "everlasting peace".
The New Testament is believed by Christians to be the
fulfillment of "Old Testament" prophecy, by which the
Messiah is "Jesus". And in Jesus, a new covenant is
made, one that accepts both Jews and non-Jews.
And that only by faith in Him, can one be
saved into "everlasting peace".

They believe that **salvation is a Gift from God**, and for one to receive this gift of salvation one must be "born of the spirit", which is accomplished by confessing to God, that you are a sinner and that nothing you do (no matter how good or how plentiful your deeds), can redeem you with God, because God is holy, and ALL have sinned (even one small sin, makes one a transgressor of the law), therefore they are unrighteous before God, for God had declared that the punishment for sin is death and because God is "just", justice must be fulfilled. So God, by His love and His Grace, begot a son, through a virgin woman named Mary, who (consumed by the Holy Spirit) gave birth to a child and named him "Jesus", Jesus is

110

believed to be the "Lamb of God", the one who bore upon himself, the punishment due to sinners and only through his sacrifice, will God grant salvation, to those who **BELIEVE IN HIS SON**. This gift of salvation is available to **ALL PEOPLE**. And those who are "SAVED", are redeemed by FAITH, they are made righteous before God, and receive eternal life in the "Kingdom of God", where God will reward everyone according to their works. Those who are not "saved" are to be judged as sinners and are subject to God's punishment (eternal separation from God, a place referred to in the Bible as "hell").

Believing in Jesus is accomplished by **loving one another.**
Jesus said "By this shall all men know that ye are my disciples, if ye have Love one to another".
(John13:35)
Jesus with regards to the law of the Jews;
"You have heard that it was said, 'Eye for eye, and tooth for tooth.' But I tell you, Do not resist an evil person.
If someone strikes you on the right cheek,
turn to him the other also."
(Matthew5:38-39)
"You have heard that it was said, 'Love your neighbor and hate your enemy.' But I tell you: Love your enemies and pray for those who persecute you, that you may be sons of your Father in heaven. He causes his sun to rise on the evil and the good, and sends rain on the righteous and the unrighteous. If you love those who love you, what reward will you get? Are not even the tax collectors doing that? And if you greet only your brothers, what are you doing more than others? Do not even pagans do that? Be perfect, therefore, as your heavenly Father is perfect."
(Matthew5:43-48)
Other sayings of Jesus
"Do not store up for yourselves treasures on earth, where moth and rust destroy, and where thieves break in and

steal. But store up for yourselves treasures in heaven, where moth and rust do not destroy, and where thieves do not break in and steal. For where your treasure is, there your heart will be also. "
(Matthew6:19-21)
"Do not judge, or you too will be judged. For in the same way you judge others, you will be judged, and with the measure you use, it will be measured to you.
Why do you look at the speck of sawdust in your brother's eye and pay no attention to the plank in your own eye? How can you say to your brother, 'Let me take the speck out of your eye,' when all the time there is a plank in your own eye? You hypocrite, first take the plank out of your own eye, and then you will see clearly to remove the speck from your brother's eye. "
(Matthew7:1-5)

THE GREATEST COMMANDMENT

"The most important one," answered Jesus, "is this: 'Hear, O Israel, the Lord our God, the Lord is one. Love the Lord your God with all your heart and with all your soul and with all your mind and with all your strength.' The second is this: 'Love your neighbor as yourself.' There is no commandment greater than these."
(Mark12:29-31)

LOVE ONE ANOTHER

"This is the message you heard from the beginning: We should love one another. Do not be like Cain, who belonged to the evil one and murdered his brother. And why did he murder him? Because his own actions were evil and his brother's were righteous. Do not be surprised, my brothers, if the world hates you. We know that we have passed from death to life, because we love our brothers. Anyone who does not love remains in death. Anyone who hates his brother is a murderer, and you know that no murderer has eternal life in him.

This is how we know what love is: Jesus Christ laid down his life for us. And we ought to lay down our lives for our brothers. If anyone has material possessions and sees his brother in need but has no pity on him, how can the love of God be in him? Dear children, let us not love with words or tongue but with actions and in truth. This then is how we know that we belong to the truth, and how we set our hearts at rest in his presence whenever our hearts condemn us. For God is greater than our hearts, and he knows everything. Dear friends, if our hearts do not condemn us, we have confidence before God and receive from him anything we ask, because we obey his commands and do what pleases him. And this is his command: to believe in the name of his Son, Jesus Christ and to love one another as he commanded us. Those who obey his commands live in him, and he in them. And this is how we know that he lives in us: We know it by the Spirit he gave us."
(John3:11-24)

Jesus lived his life as fully man and fully God,
he was tempted by the desires of the flesh, he was
tempted by Satan, yet he remained pure and sinless. Jesus
performed a great deal of miracles such as making the blind
see, healing the sick, walking on water, and even raising
the dead. Jesus spoke that he was "born into the world,
not to judge it but to save it by being a sacrifice for sin".
He also proclaimed that in His blood, is a new
covenant, one not made on tablets of
stone but on human hearts.

Christians believe that three days after the death of Jesus, he came back to life and told his followers to spread the "good news" of his resurrection and victory over sin. Jesus then ascended into Heaven, promising that one day he will return and his kingdom will reign forever.

113

My Personal Views on Christianity are:

_____

_____

_____

_____

_____

_____

_____

_____

_____

_____

_____

_____

_____

_____

The religion of Hinduism believes:

Different religions lead to the same God.
It is perhaps one of the most complicated religions to grasp,
because it has no founder and no established beginning,
this leads to vast array of interpretations that depend upon,
how one chooses to view Hinduism.
Being such,
Hinduism can be considered
Polytheistic (belief in many Gods),
or **Monotheistic** (belief in one God).
Some even contest that Hinduism is
Pantheistic (which means "God is All" and "All is God")
or **Atheistic** (which rejects a creator or "God", due to the
dual existence of Prakriti "nature" and Purusha "spirit",
thus having no place for a Ishvara (which is "God").
So who is to say which is right and which is wrong?
THE BELIEVER
(It is open to how one perceives it)
The most common Hindu philosophy is the belief in one
God, "Brahman" who appears in millions of ways, because
for us to comprehend "one" Supreme Being (with our
limited intellect) is impossible. So to help us, the infinite,
manifests "himself", into nearly an infinite amount of
divisions, so that we *may be able* to conceive of him. These
divisions are represented in numerous deities (gods), which
are often depicted as statues or idols. Each "holy" statue is
believed to symbolize a various "aspect" of Brahman.
Although these **idols** are considered "holy", they are
recognized by believers, as being no more than clay
and paint, and worship given to such idols, are
meant towards, the specific "nature" in which
the symbol represents Brahman.
It is believed that worshipers gain "spiritual merit", through
offerings (such as food or gifts), to the idol of their choice.

Hindus perform this ritual, as a devotion to a "Deva God", and it is believed that the deity absorbs the "essence" of the food, this is known as **"Puja"**.

(Please Note: Many Buddhist also perform "Puja", before "Buddhist statues", and do so only out of tradition, because the original "Buddha" taught, that such rituals, do nothing).

Other than offering food during Puja, one may offer water, flowers, incense, chanting, candles, sound of a bell, a waving of a fan, or even the sounding a conch-shell.

Other popular practices include
YOGA and MEDITATION.

Many Hindus create shrines with numerous idols/deities, dedicated to the individual's particular favorite "God".

Some of the better-known deities include
Krishna, Ganesha, Parvati, Lakshmi, and Indra.

"GANESHA"
is believed to be
the remover of obstacles, God of prosperity and wisdom.
According to legend·
Ganesha grew up with out knowing his father "SHIVA".
And one day while Ganesha was standing guard as his mother (Parvati) bathed, Shiva had returned and requested to be let in. Ganesha (not knowing who Shiva was) stood his ground and refused to move, so Shiva became very angry and cut off Ganesha's head, only to discover later, that he had killed his own son. So Shiva replaced his son's head, with the first live creature that passed (an elephant).
Shiva then decreed,
that no prayer would begin without invoking Ganesha.

Three of the "main" Hindu gods are,
BRAHMA (who is the creator) **VISHNU** (the preserver,
who maintains the universe) and **SHIVA** (the destroyer,
agent of death and destruction), each represent a
"nature" of Brahman.

Hindus believe in
KARMA and REINCARNATION
Since the soul is considered the "essential nature of
everyone", it is believed to perpetually cycle (in death and
rebirth). **Reincarnation** takes place every time you die;
you are then born into another **living creature**, based upon
your accumulated **Karma.** Those who do good receive
good Karma (positive blessings in the next life) and those
who do bad, receive bad Karma (thus will be cursed in the
next life). Suffering in the present life, is the mere result
of bad Karma, from your previous life.
To free oneself from this cycle (of suffering and rebirth),
and return to Brahman is the Hindus "purpose in life"
(also known as Moksha, Nirvana or Samadhi).

"To Each Their Own"
Hindu's believe each person is free to believe as they
choose (so long as you don't hurt anybody). They are
encouraged to develop their faith through experience. They
believe that it is best to follow one's own **"Dharma"**
perfectly, than to follow another's imperfectly. **"Sanatana
Dharma"** which is better known as Hinduism, is not only a
religion, but a way of life, and that one must follow the
path that is right for them. This path is found through the
law of Dharma (the right way of living), and to find
this path, one only has to only look within.

Hinduism has "given birth" to many other religions; such as
Buddhism, the Jain and Sikh religions.

"Many Scriptures - Many Paths"
They have sacred scriptures,
that help instruct and guide them,
such as **the Vedas and the Upanishads.**
Some other scriptures include the Tantras, the Purā□as, the
Mahābhārata (which incorporates "The Bhagavad Gītā"
and is believed to be written by Ganesha) and Rāmāya□a,
again they remain to be, what they are,
to those who read them.

Hinduism is more so a philosophy of life,
than a religion,
it is knowledge handed down over thousands of years.

Most devout Hindus believe:
The life of a cow is more important than the life of a man.

That man made medicine goes against God's will,
for if one is sick, it is because of lack of faith
and "God willed" for them be so.

That the Gangee's river is the purest water
in all the world and that bathing in
it waters, removes all sins
and cures all diseases.

No one can accurately depict the religion of Hinduism,
because what it is to one believer,
it is not to another.

IT IS A "SO BE IT" RELIGION,
AS YOU BELIEVE IT,
SO BE IT.

My Personal Views on Hinduism are:

_____

_____

_____

_____

_____

_____

_____

_____

_____

_____

_____

_____

_____

_____

_____

The religion of Islam believes:

Islam means "submission to the will of God".
A **Muslim** is one who "submits to the will of God".
They believe in **"Allah"** (personal name of God)
and declare Islam
"The path of those upon whom Thou hast bestowed favors.
Not those upon whom wrath is brought down (such as the
Jews), nor those who go astray (such as the Christians)."
(Surah 1:6-7).
They believe that the "Old Testament" of the Jews and the
"New Testament" of the Christians were intended to be
true, but became corrupted by those of who wrote them.
Around the year 630 A.D.,
Allah sent the Archangel Gabriel, who appeared before
Muhammad and commanded him to write nothing, but
what was recited to him. Now Muhammad was illiterate not
being able to read or write, but Allah used Muhammad to
write His word, which formed the book known as the
"Koran" and it is believed that the Koran can only be read
"properly" if it is read in its original language, Arabic.
Therefore being that I quote the Koran in English (so that
you may be able to read it), please know that it is not
"perfectly accurate" because it is not done so in Arabic.
Because Muhammad was not able to read or write,
Muslims believe that Allah used the hand of Muhammad
thus "guaranteeing the perfectness" of the final result,
the "Noble Koran", and **every word within the**
Koran is believed to be the direct
revelation of Allah.
Being such, they believe it is infallible (without error) and
the most perfect book ever written in the world.
The Koran claims that only the religion of Islam is the one
true religion. **Muslims must testify, there is no God,**
but God, and Muhammad is his Prophet.

Muhammad is the **descendant of Ishmael**, son of Abraham
(as in the "Old Testament"). Muhammad is believed to be
the "seal" of all the Prophets, and none will follow.
Abraham,
Ishmael, Isaac,
Noah, Moses, David,
Jonah, Elijah, Jeremiah,
Nathan, Zechariah, John the Baptist,
and Jesus, are ALL "predecessors of Muhammad",
they are all considered equal "messengers of God."
*"...we do not make any distinction between any of them
and to Him (Allah) do we submit."*
(2:136, see also 3:83)
Muhammad
"peace be upon him"
(Muslims say this, after his name, as a term of respect),
Muhammad is the last and final Prophet.
There is no need for more prophets, because
Allah's message is complete in the Koran.

Some beliefs in Islam,
*"And whoever obeys Allah and the Messenger,
they are with those upon whom Allah has bestowed favors
from among the prophets and the truthful and the faithful
and the righteous, and a goodly company are they!"*
(4:69)
*"Surely the vilest of beasts in Allah's sight
are those who disbelieve, then would not believe."*
(8:55)
*"Evil is the likeness of the people who reject
Our messages and wrong their own souls."*
(7:177)
*"And those who disbelieve and reject Our message,
such are the companions of the flaming fire."*
(5:86)

121

"And they are enjoined naught but to serve Allah, being sincere to Him in obedience, upright, and to keep up the poor-rate, and that is the right religion."
(98:5)
"Muhammad brings the truth, those who believe will enter paradise, those who disbelieve enter hell fire."
(2:119)

The Koran
with regards to fighting in defense
"And fight in the way of Allah against those who fight against you but be not aggressive. Surely Allah loves not the aggressors. And kill them wherever you find them, and drive them out from where they drove you out, and persecution (Fitnah = disbelief in Allah) is worse than slaughter (killing). And fight not with them at the Sacred Mosque until they fight with you in it; so if they fight you, slay them. Such is the recompense of the disbelievers."
(2:190-191)
"And fight them until there is no persecution, and religion is only for Allah. But if they desist, then there should be no hostility except against oppressors.
...Whoever then acts aggressively against you, inflict injury on him according to the injury he has inflicted on you and keep duty to Allah, and know that Allah is with those who keep their duty"
(2:193-194)

The Koran
with regards to befriending non-Muslims (during war)
"O you who believe, take not the disbelievers for friends rather than the believers. Do you desire to give Allah a manifest proof against yourselves?"
(4:144)

122

"O you who believe, take not the Jews and the Christians for friends. They are friends of each other. **And whoever amongst you takes them for friends he is indeed one of them.** *Surely Allah guides not the unjust people."*
(5:51)
"O you who believe, take not My enemy and your enemy for friends. **Would you offer them love, while they deny the Truth that has come to you,** *driving out the Messenger and yourselves because you believe in Allah you Lord? If you have come forth to strive in My way and to seek My pleasure, would you love them in secret? And I know what you conceal and what you manifest. And whoever of you does this, he indeed strays from the straight path."*
(60:1)

The Koran
With regards to Christians and the Jews
"O People of the Book, exceed not the limits in your religion nor speak anything about Allah, but the truth. The Messiah, **Jesus, son of Mary, is only a messenger of Allah** *and His word which He communicated to Mary and a mercy from Him. So Believe in Allah and His messengers. And say not, Three. Desist, it is better for you. Allah is only one God. Far be it from His glory to have a son. To Him belongs whatever is in the heavens and whatever is in the earth. And sufficient is Allah as having charge of affairs."*
(4:171)
"And say: Praise be to Allah! Who has not taken to Himself a son, and Who has not a partner in the kingdom, and Who has not a helper because of weakness; and proclaim His greatness, magnifying (Him)."
(17:111)
"These our people have taken gods beside Him. Why do

they not bring clear authority for them? Who is then more unjust than he who forges a lie against Allah?"
(18:15)
"Those who disbelieve from among the People of the Book and the idolaters will be in the Fire of hell, abiding therein. They are the worst of creatures."
(98:6)
"...Surely We have prepared hell as an entertainment for the disbelievers (Christians)."
(18:102)
"Accursed, wherever they are found they will be seized and slain. That was the way of Allah concerning those who have gone before; and thou wilt find no change in the way of Allah."
(33:61-62)
"Surely Allah has cursed the unbelievers and has prepared for them a burning fire, To abide therein for a long time; they shall not find a protector or a helper."
(33:64-65)
"Now surely it is of their own lie that they say: Allah has begotten. And truly they are liars."
(37:151-152)
"And whoever believes not in Allah and His Messenger – then surely We have prepared burning fire for disbelievers.
(48:13)
"So let those fight in the way of Allah who sell this world's life for the Hereafter. And whoever fights in the way of Allah, be he slain or be he victorious, We shall grant him a mighty reward." (72 virgins)
(4:74)
"O you who believe, fight those of the disbelievers who are near to you and let them find firmness in you. And know that Allah is with those who keep their duty."
(9:123)
"Those who believe fight in the way of Allah, and those

124

who disbelieve fight in the way of the devil. So fight
against the friends of the devil; surely the struggle
of the devil is ever weak."
(4:76)
"Fight those who believe not in Allah, nor in the Last Day,
nor forbid that which Allah and His Messenger have
forbidden, nor follow the Religion of Truth, out of
those who have been given the Book, until they
pay tax in acknowledgement of superiority and
they are in a state of subjection."
(9:29)
"So when you meet in battle
those who disbelieve (such as the Jews and Christians),
smite the necks; then, when you have overcome them, make
(them) prisoners... And **those who are slain in the way of**
Allah, He will never allow their deeds to perish.*"*
(47:4)

The Koran
with regards to Allah,
"He it is Who has sent His Messenger (Muhammad) with
the guidance and the religion of Truth that He may make it
prevail over all religions. And Allah is enough
for a witness."
(48:28)
"And those who believe in Allah and His messenger, they
are the truthful and faithful ones with their Lord. They have
their reward and their light. And those who disbelieve and
reject Our messages, they are the inmates of hell."
(57:19)
"It may be that Allah will bring about friendship between
you and those of them whom you hold as enemies. And
Allah is Powerful; and Allah is Forgiving, Merciful."
(60:7)
"Allah forbids you not respecting those who fight you not

125

for religion... Allah forbids you only respecting those who
fight you for religion... "
(60:8-9)

In Islam
Any worship or prayers directed towards
Saints, Prophets, or Jesus is considered idolatry.

Every believer must perform five holy duties,
known as:
"The Five Pillars"
Foremost is **Confession of Faith**
testify that there is no God except for Allah,
and Muhammad is his messenger. This must be
declared with purity of heart and conviction of faith.
The second is **Prayer**, five times a day (facing the Kaaba).
The third is **Fasting**, in the month of Ramadan, the month
which was sent down the Qur'an.
Fourth is **Almsgiving**, Muslims who are financially able,
are to give 2.5% of their earnings to the needy.
The fifth and final duty is the **Pilgrimage to Mecca**.

They believe the first house of worship was **Mecca**, where
Abraham built the **Kaaba,** for which all Muslims
face during their daily prayers. A Pilgrimage
there is a duty men owe to Allah, for
those who can afford the journey.
In Mecca,
all people stand before Allah as equals.

The words "Islam" and "Muslim"
derive from the Arabic word
for "peace".

There is no priesthood in Islam.

126

Forbidden to Muslims is:
dishonesty, theft, murder, interest, gambling, consumption
of alcohol or pork, cruelty to animals, adultery, improper
exposure of the body (in public, no man should
expose his body from the navel to the knees
and women should not expose any part
of her body except her face and hands.
This covering, cultivates a sense of
modesty, purity and respect.

Muslims only kill under the belief
that it is the "will of Allah".

Muslims do not believe that Jesus died, was killed,
or was crucified, but that he ascended into heaven alive.

Most Muslim countries
are dictatorships with restricted human rights,
and severely oppress women. The Koran promotes
Muslim men to marry up to four wives.

Muslims believe that abundant good deeds
or killing in defense of Islam,
is the way in to heaven.

**If a Muslim converts to a different faith,
the punishment is to be death.**

Jihad represents the battle of submitting one's will to Allah
or it is also known as "holy war" which is a sacred duty.

**Islam has widespread rejection of Israel and it's
supporters, such as the U.S.A. (aka "The Great Satan").**
Approximately 20% of all people on earth follow Islam,
approximately 1 billion worldwide.

My Personal Views on Islam are:

_____

_____

_____

_____

_____

_____

_____

_____

_____

_____

_____

_____

_____

The religion of Judaism believes:

"HEAR, O ISRAEL:
THE HaShem OUR GOD, THE HaShem IS ONE.
And thou shalt love HaShem thy G-d with all thy heart,
and with all thy soul, and with all thy might.
(Jewish Bible Deuteronomy 6:4-5)
They believe they are descendents of
Abraham, Isaac, and Jacob.
"And G-d said unto him: 'Thy name is Jacob:
thy name shall not be called any more Jacob, but Israel
*shall be thy name'; and He called his name **Israel.'***
So he named him Israel."
(Jewish Bible Genesis 35:10)

Descendents of Israel are known as "Israelites".

"Then Moses went up to God, and the LORD called to him
from the mountain and said, 'This is what you are to say to
the house of Jacob and what you are to tell the people of
Israel: 'You yourselves have seen what I did to Egypt, and
how I carried you on eagles' wings and brought you to
*myself. Now **if you obey me fully and keep my covenant,***
then out of all nations you will be my treasured possession.
Although the whole earth is mine, you will be for me a
kingdom of priests and a holy nation.' These are the
words you are to speak to the Israelites."
(Exodus 19:3-6)

God's Chosen People

Israelites believe they are descendents of Abraham, who
was promised by God, that if he left his comfortable life,
he would become the father of a great nation. Even though
Abraham and his wife Sarah, were not young and had no
children, he accepted the call. Sarah, believing she was to

old to bare a child, convinced her husband into having a child through her slave woman. Thus, Ishmael was born, but he was not to be the heir of Gods promise. Sarah, at a very old age bore Abraham a son, Isaac. **God made a covenant (a conditional promise) with Abraham and promised him, that He would protect and preserve Abraham's family, that they would be as numerous as the stars of heaven, and they would be his Chosen People. (Found in Genesis 17)**

WHY ABRAHAM?
God chose Abraham because
Abraham broke away from the pagan worship of his time
and believed in the *oneness of God*.
God chose Abraham, because Abraham chose God.

They believe in the
TEN COMMANDMENTS
1. I am the Lord your God
2. Thou shall have no other gods before me, nor make for yourself an idol
3. Thou shall not make wrongful use of the name of your God
4. Remember the Sabbath and keep it holy
5. Honor your parents
6. Thou shall not murder
7. Thou shall not commit adultery
8. Thou shall not steal
9. Thou shall not bear false witness.
10. You shall not covet your neighbor's house; you shall not covet your neighbor's wife, nor anything that is your neighbor's.

Believers judge everything under the law.
They believe that God will reward those who keep His commandments and punish those who transgress them.

130

Sin Offering

When one disobeys any of these commandments, forgiveness is made by presenting a live animal, making atonement over it (where one lays both hands on an animal and confesses their sins over it, this transfer's the iniquities onto the animal) and then they kill it. This is known as a **"sin offering"**, and is believed to cleanse one; from all their sins, thus making them clean before the Lord.

According to the Law

The following is a partial list of **some of the sins that are to be punished by death:** anyone who **kills,** must be put to death (unless it was an accident), anyone **who strikes father or mother** must be put to death, **kidnappers** must be killed, anyone who **curses father or mother** must be put to death. An **adulterous** is to be stoned to death. **Idolatry, blasphemy, consulting a medium, unlawful divorce, homosexuality, incest, Sabbath violations, bestiality, prostitution of virgins, the practice of magic, and false prophesying,** anyone who does these must be put to death (according to the law). If an eye is injured, injure the eye of the person who did it. If a tooth gets knocked out, knock out the tooth of the person who did it. Payment must be hand in hand, foot for foot, burn for burn, wound for wound, bruise for bruise (most of this is found in Exodus 21 the rest is found scattered in the Torah).

Their holy book is called the **T'nakh**
which consists of the **Torah** (the five books of Moses)
Genesis, Exodus, Leviticus, Numbers and Deuteronomy,
Two remaining parts are called **Neviim** "the Prophets",
and **Ketuvim** "the writings".
(Christians call these books the "Old Testament" a name they gave it, because they believe that the Bible of the Jews was taken away and superseded by a newer version, hence the name "New Testament".)

131

With regards to the Messiah:
They do not believe Jesus was the Messiah
(announced by prophecy, nor the son of God),
for he equated himself with God.
They solely believe **God is one**, for God says in the T'nakh
"I am the Lord your God", and
"You shall have no other Gods before Me."

KINGDOM OF GOD
**Judaism believes that one enters heaven by deserving it,
through obedience to His Law.**

Judaism put an emphasis on a **God of Law**.
For it is through His law that one learns how to be holy.
When a believer dies, those who are over abundant in good
deeds are inscribed in God's *book of Life,* and those
who are wicked, their fate is sealed in the
book for *Death and Misfortune.*
Although,
most believers are somewhere in the middle, and for them,
God grants a *last chance*, ten days to improve, to better
their lives and commit to His law. It is on this tenth day,
the day of **Yom Kippur**, God will conclude
whether or not one deserves *atonement.*
This is known as
Ten Days of Repentance.

Other beliefs common in Judaism:
They believe in a coming Messiah that will
gather Jews once more into the land of Israel.

They believe that the Jerusalem Temple
(that was destroyed in the year 70A.D.) will be rebuilt.

And they believe one day the dead will be resurrected.

132

My Personal Views on Judaism are:

_____

_____

_____

_____

_____

_____

_____

_____

_____

_____

_____

_____

_____

_____

Is it Possible to Save Oneself?
NO
Because *sin* makes it *impossible*, **for we are all sinners,**
corrupt and unclean and **God is Holy, Holy, Holy**, and it's
because of *His Righteousness, sin must be punished.*
"True Christians" believe that punishment was paid
for (in full), by the sacrifice of Jesus Christ.
But if you have ever wondered why a
Loving God would have His son
Sacrificed to pay that price,
Please permit me to explain.
The following explanation is not a personal point of view,
but reasoning expressed through the Bible (Gods Word).
With that being said, I will do the best I can, to explain.
Keep in mind, that these will be just "some" of the
key reasons, and for a "fuller understanding"
one should read the Bible. This is not really
the kind of question, that should be
answered briefly, but again I
will do my best.
First,
Before one can understand WHY,
they must understand some history with regards to the
OLD COVENANT
(a conditional promise made to humanity by God)
Briefly,
God created man and placed him in the Garden of Eden,
He instructed Adam that he may eat the fruit, from all the
tree's except one, for if he ate the fruit from
"The Tree of Knowledge" he would surely die.
Adam committed the one sin God spoke of,
causing God to curse man and the earth.
Mankind gained the knowledge of "good and evil",
but lost "innocence" and became "corrupted".
Remember that God said "the punishment for sin is death".

134

Hundreds of years later,
a descendent of Adam, named **"Abram"**, believed in the
Oneness of God, an uncommon belief at the time,
for the world had become very sinful and
polytheistic (belief in many gods).
So,
"God told Abram to leave the land he was living in
and that The LORD had said to Abram, "Leave your
country, your people and your father's household and
go to the land I will show you. "I will make you into
a great nation and I will bless you; I will make your
name great, and you will be a blessing. I will bless those
who bless you, and whoever curses you I will curse;
and all peoples on earth will be blessed through you. "
So Abram left, as the LORD had told him... "
(Genesis12:1-4)
"Abram believed the LORD,
and He credited it to him as righteousness. "
(Genesis15:6)
God told Abram,
"...You will be the father of many nations. No longer will
*you be called Abram; your name will be **Abraham**, for I*
*have made you **a father of many nations. "***
(Genesis17:4-5)
Then God said,
...your wife Sarah will bear you a son, and you will call
*him Isaac. I will establish **my covenant** with him as **an***
***everlasting covenant** for his descendants after him.*
(Genesis17:19)
Later on,
God tests Abraham's faith and obedience,
by asking Abraham to sacrifice his son, Isaac.
Abraham obeyed Gods command, and just before Abraham
was about to slay his son, an angel of the LORD, stops him.
(This can be read in Genesis chapter 22)

The angel then spoke,
"Do not lay a hand on the boy," he said. "Do not do
anything to him. Now I know that you fear God, <u>because</u>
<u>*you have not withheld from me your son, your only son.*</u>*"*
Abraham looked up and there in a thicket he saw a ram
caught by its horns. He went over and took the ram and
sacrificed it as a burnt offering instead of his son.
Abraham called that place **The LORD Will Provide.**
<u>*And to this day it is said,*</u>
<u>*"On the mountain of the LORD it will be provided."*</u>
The angel of the LORD called to Abraham from heaven a
second time and said, "I swear by myself, declares the
LORD, <u>that because you have done this and have not</u>
<u>*withheld your son, your only son, I will surely bless you*</u>*
and make your descendants as numerous as the stars in the*
sky and as the sand on the seashore. Your descendants will
take possession of the cities of their enemies, and through
your offspring all nations on earth will be blessed,
because you have obeyed me."
(Genesis22:12-18)
Some time later,
Isaac bore a son named **Jacob***,*
whom God saw fit to change his name
"...Your name will no longer be Jacob, but **"Israel"***,*
because you have struggled with God and
with men and have overcome."
(Genesis32:28)

God then tells Israel,
"And God said to him, 'I am God Almighty; be fruitful and
increase in number. A nation and a community of nations
will come from you, and kings will come from your body.
The land I gave to Abraham and Isaac I also give to you,
and I will give this land to your descendants after you'."
(Genesis35:11)

136

Centuries later,
"Then Moses went up to God, and the LORD called to him
from the mountain and said, 'This is what you are to say to
the house of Jacob and what you are to tell the people of
Israel: You yourselves have seen what I did to Egypt, and
how I carried you on eagles' wings and brought you to
myself. Now if you obey me fully and keep my covenant,
then out of all nations you will be my treasured possession.
Although the whole earth is mine, you will be for me a
kingdom of priests and a holy nation. These are the
words you are to speak to the Israelites'."
(Exodus19:3-6)
Then,
God gives Moses the 10 Commandments.
(found in Exodus chapter 20)
So,
"Moses then took the blood, sprinkled it on the people and
said, "This is the blood of the covenant that the LORD has
made with you in accordance with all these words."
(Exodus24:8)
"The LORD said to Moses,
"Come up to me on the mountain and stay here, and I
will give you the tablets of stone, with the law and
commands I have written for their instruction."
(Exodus24:12)
Quick Recap:
so far we've learned
that God has made a **covenant**,
that "IF" they obey His commandments,
He will make them, His treasured possession, a holy nation
(understand this is all subject to them keeping His law).
Now
a covenant is made in blood,
"In the case of a will, it is necessary to prove the death of
the one who made it, because a will is in force only when

137

somebody has died; it never takes effect while the one who made it is living. This is why even the first covenant was not put into effect without blood. When Moses had proclaimed every commandment of the law to all the people, he took the blood of calves, together with water, scarlet wool and branches of hyssop, and sprinkled the scroll and all the people. He said, "This is the blood of the covenant, which God has commanded you to keep." In the same way, he sprinkled with the blood both the tabernacle and everything used in its ceremonies. In fact, the law requires that nearly everything be cleansed with blood, and **without the shedding of blood there is no forgiveness.**
(Hebrews9:16-22)

Well
the Israelites, were unfaithful to God and continuously broke His laws. So rather than just wiping them all out, He showed compassion and created a
NEW COVENANT
God declares,
"For if there had been nothing wrong with that first covenant, no place would have been sought for another.
But God found fault with the people and said:
'The time is coming, declares the Lord,
when I will make a **new covenant** *with the house of Israel and with the house of Judah. It will not be like the covenant I made with their forefathers when I took them by the hand to lead them out of Egypt, because* <u>they did not remain faithful to my covenant</u>, *and I turned away from them, declares the Lord. This is the covenant I will make with the house of Israel after that time, declares the Lord. I will put my laws in their minds and write them on their hearts.*
I will be their God, and they will be my people.
No longer will a man teach his neighbor,
or a man his brother, saying, "Know the Lord,"

138

*because they will all know me, from the least of them to the greatest. **For I will forgive their wickedness and will remember their sins no more.'** By calling this covenant **"new,"** he has made the first one obsolete; and what is obsolete and aging will soon disappear."*
(Hebrews8:7-13)
Now in order for God to forgive their sins,
a sacrifice must be made in it's place.
Remember **God is a "Just God"**
therefore sin must **ABSOLUTLEY** be punished.
God cannot just forget about sin, because He had said
the punishment for sin is death, and His word is Truth,
so punishment must come to pass, or He would not
be speaking Truth (and there is no lie in Him).

Redemption
*"For Christ did not enter a man-made sanctuary that was only a copy of the true one; he entered heaven itself, now to appear for us in God's presence. Nor did he enter heaven to offer himself again and again, the way the high priest enters the Most Holy Place every year with blood that is not his own. Then Christ would have had to suffer many times since the creation of the world. But now he has appeared once for all at the end of the ages **to do away with sin by the sacrifice of himself.** Just as man is destined to die once, and after that to face judgment, so Christ was sacrificed once **to take away the sins of many people;** and he will appear a second time, not to bear sin, but **to bring salvation** to those who are waiting for him."*
(Hebrews9:24-28)

The Mediator
"For this reason Christ is the mediator of a new covenant, that those who are called may receive the promised eternal inheritance—now that he has died as a ransom to set them free from the sins committed under the first covenant."
(Hebrews9:15)

139

"In the same way, after the supper he took the cup, saying,
'This cup is the_new covenant in my blood, which is
poured out for you'."
(Luke 22:20)

It's important to understand that,
Jesus gave his life freely nobody took it from him,
but he willingly gave his life as a ransom for ALL our sins.
Through his sacrifice the Law is now fulfilled.
For sin has been severely punished,
just as God proclaimed it must
(IN DEATH).
Three days after the death of Jesus,
he comes back to life, appears before hundreds of his
followers and tells them **to spread the good news.**

So according to the Bible,
every person has a choice to make,
they can **accept the gift of salvation**
(given to us by the grace and love of God),
Or
They can choose to **go before the judgment seat,**
as a sinner and transgressor of the law,
where they will be judged upon
righteously. God left the
decision entirely
up to you.

Sin has divided all of us from God,
but through God's amazing love for us, He has provided
redemption through His son, so that anyone who
"believes upon him, shall have eternal life".
To accept Gods gift of salvation,
one only has to repent of their sins and believe in Jesus.

Why do you believe there is a God?

_____

_____

_____

_____

_____

_____

_____

_____

What Doubts do you have that hinder your faith?

_____

_____

_____

_____

_____

What is the difference between
"Catholic" and "Protestant" Christianity?

*It would be like comparing the light of
the moon, to the light of the sun.*

First understand,
The Catholic Church is the single largest denomination
in Christianity, but most Christians are Protestant.
If this is confusing, I will simplify it in terms of money
(because nearly everyone understands money).
If you have thirty percent of your stock in one
mutual fund, and the remaining seventy
percent dispersed in smaller accounts,
the largest fund in your portfolio
would be the fund that
has thirty percent.
Right?
But "most" of your money is in all the other mutual funds
for they make up seventy percent of your portfolio.
Well
the same goes for the population of Christians,
the biggest denomination in Christianity, is Catholic,
but the majority of Christians are Protestant.

The word "Protestant"
derives from the word "protest",
Protestant Christians, are Christians who have rejected
the authority of the Pope and his church.
Protestant and Catholic are two forms of Christianity.
But to simplify this,
Protestants are generally referred to as "Christians"
and
Roman Catholics are usually referred to as "Catholics"

During the time of Jesus, the Roman Empire was in power, years after the death of Jesus, the Roman Government came to believe in Jesus and thus was formed, what is known today as the "Roman Catholic Church"

Around the year 1500
The Church and its popes had become incredibly powerful, more so than all the kings and rulers of its time; they were extremely wealthy and so powerful, that they ultimately became corrupt. The Church was HUGE business, so big in fact, that they even started selling something they called "indulgences" the priests would then sell these indulgences, claiming that any sin could be forgiven for the right price (if you are surprised by that, the history of the Church of Rome would absolutely blow you away). The Church was making so much money with these indulgences, that they started selling them for future sins, that is if one knew they were going to commit a sin, they could buy an "indulgence" (a Catholic form of a "get out of hell free card". If you're Catholic and becoming offended by this, first let me state that this is not my opinion, this is fact, the history of the Church was at best detestable, and although I could easily fill a massive book covering the atrocities practiced by the early Church, it is not my intention to do so. I only want to introduce *some* of the differences between Catholic and Protestant theology.

NOTE: If you are interested in learning more about the history of the early Roman Catholic Church, there are many informative books written on this matter, just be prepared, it's known as "The Dark Ages" for good reason.

Martin Luther (not to be mistaken with Dr. Martin Luther King Jr., but this is who Dr. King was named after, sorry some may not know this), Martin Luther was once a member of the clergy within the church. Appalled by the corruption within the church, Martin Luther spoke up and pleaded for the church to once again stand for Jesus, and not for "itself". Needless to say, his criticism wasn't taken well and he was booted out of the church, so he did what he felt was right and began preaching, not from the authority of the church, but from the authority of the Bible alone. Now there were many other clergymen who criticized the Church of Rome, but history shows none of them had an impact like Martin Luther's, his revolt brought a reformation know as;

"Protestant Christianity"
Those who no longer accepted the authority
of the Roman Catholic church, but granted all authority
to the Bible only.

Now the important question here is
How are they different?
Well the Catholic Church "officially" accepts the Bible as the inspired Word of God. But the problem (according to Protestants) is that **many** beliefs which the Catholic Church adheres to, is not in agreement with the Bible.
So,
I will explain a course
of the Catholic Church, then actual scripture from the Holy Bible, which "Both" Catholics and Christians believe in, then you can make any conclusions for yourself.

AUTHORITY:
Catholicism grants "final authority" to the Church, this means that any declarations made by **Popes and Councils**, is considered to be equally authoritative as the Bible.
AND

144

Protestant Christians grant all authority to **the Bible.**
Just about every difference
between the two, stems from this.

DEFINITION:
Roman Catholic Church
"When you're fully incorporated into the society of the **church**, who possessing the spirit of Christ, **accept its entire system and all means of salvation** given to it, and through union with its visible structure are joined to Christ, who rules it through the **Supreme Pontiff**, which is the **Pope** and the bishops. This joining is effected by the bonds of professed faith, of the **Sacraments**, of ecclesiastical government, and of communion."

Protestant Christianity
One who **believes in the Bible** *and does not adhere to the methods of the Roman Catholic Church.*

MARY:
The **Catholic Church** refers to Mary as the "Redemtrix" a
Co-Redeemer, they believe in praying to her (this idea is
not supported anywhere throughout scripture).
According to the Bible,
the only command Mary ever gives about Jesus,
is when she says,
"...Do whatever he tells you."
(John 2:5)

Catholics believe that it is not only "permissible", but also
"profitable" to venerate Mary.
**Catholics make mediators to God,
through Mary, the Church, the Clergy,
Angels and the Saints.**

145

The Bible reads,
*"God is one. **One also is the mediator between
God and men, the man Christ Jesus** who
gave himself as a ransom for all."*
(1Timothy 2:5)
Jesus in his own words says, *"I am the way, the truth, and
the life, <u>no one comes to the Father, but through me</u>"*
(John 14:6)
The Bible never mentions, nor even insinuates that Mary
should be viewed upon as a "co-redeemer".
In fact,
Jesus barely mentions His mother in the Bible,
and when He does, He in no way suggests that she is to be
worshiped or prayed to. The first attempt of glorifying
Mary is even found in the Bible, when a woman yells out
from a crowd, to Jesus saying,
"Blest is the womb that bore you and the
breasts that nursed you."
**Which Jesus replied "Rather, blest are they who
hear the word of God and keep it"**
(Luke 11:27)

Another time,
Jesus was told that his Mother
came to visit him, outside, which he replies
"Who is my Mother? Who are my brothers?"
Then he points to his followers and says,
*"**My true brother and sister and mother
are those who do what my father in heaven wants**".*
(Matthew12:46 and Mark 3:31).

Protestant Christians do not believe
Mary is a "Co-Redeemer"
They believe there is only **one mediator** between
God and men, the man **Christ Jesus**.

146

GOVERNED BY:

The **Catholic Church** is governed by ecclesiastical rulers (also known as a **"hierarchy"** where supreme power is vested in the **Pope and the council)**. For Catholics, all truth is dictated by the Pope, therefore **freethinking and opposition is not admitted.**

It is not possible to be good Catholic
and think differently than
the Pope or the Church.

For every true Catholic
according to **"dogma"**, that is Catholic law,
must acknowledge the **infallibility** (perfect-ness) of the
Pope, and that what he says, is not from him, but a direct
revelation from Jesus. To think differently is defiance to the
Church. *(Yet, even a mediocre attempt to study the history
of the Roman Church, would uncover numerous errors,
contradictions, and apologies performed by the Church).*
According to **Catholic Church**, the Church began with the
apostle Peter, who was "personally" selected by Jesus,
to establish the church (found in Matthew 16:18).
Catholics claim their "popes" to be successors of Peter.

Protestant Christians also claim that the church began
with Peter, but "do not" believe him to be infallible.
The Bible says,
*"Just moments after Jesus declared Peter, to lead the
church, Peter says something that appalled Jesus,
so much so that Jesus yells at Peter saying*
"Go away from me, Satan!
*You don't care about the things of God,
but only about the things,
man thinks is important"*
(Matthew 16:22).

Protestant Christians assert that,
if the Bible says, that Peter, was in no way "infallible",
then how can Popes (who "claim" to be successors of
Peter), suddenly become infallible?
To do so CONTRADICTS THE BIBLE
plus,
there's no Biblical reasoning to support the idea that Peter's
authority, was ever to be passed on (let alone to Popes).
The Pope,
claims the right to
have men bow down to them,
now the Bible says, that when Peter
(whom the popes claim to be descendents of),
"when Peter entered, Cornelius met him, fell at his
feet and worshiped him, but Peter helped him up
saying, stand up, I too am only human"
(Acts 10;25)

Never did Peter suggest or insinuate that he is to be looked
upon as superior. The Bible says, that man
is not to be bowed to, nor even angels
(yet the Pope declared his "infallibility" in 1870).

Protestant Christianity
Is not governed by a hierarchy, they believe
each individual has the right to interpret the Bible.
Being that people are different, they interpret
some things differently (and this is why so many
denominations exist within Christianity).

SALVATION:
The **Catholic Church**
Adheres to a "method" for achieving
salvation through what they call
"The Seven Sacraments"

The Seven Sacraments are:

Baptism, which cleans one from original sin.
Confirmation where you receive the Holy Spirit.
Eucharist, is the "true body and blood" of Jesus.
Penance, where sins committed after baptism are forgiven.
Anointing of the sick, where the sick are anointed with holy oil, accompanied with prayer.
Holy orders, is the sacrament which the bishops, priests, and deacons of the church are ordained, and receive power and grace to perform their sacred duties.
Matrimony, which sanctifies the contract of a Christian marriage.
These sacraments are believed to "bestow grace", and one obtains God's grace, through prayer and these holy sacraments.

Protestant Christianity

Not only will you not find the word **"seven sacraments"** any where in the Bible, but just the implication that one has to perform any such sacrament, in order to obtain salvation, **completely contradicts Jesus.**
The Bible says,
" *that **everyone who believes in him** may have eternal life For God so loved the world that he gave his one and only Son, that whoever believes in him shall not perish but have eternal life. For **God** did not send his **Son** into the world to condemn the world, but to **save the world through him** "*
(John 3:15-17)
Jesus said, "Your faith has saved you; go in peace."
(Luke 7:50)
*"Jesus said, I am the resurrection and the life. **He who believes in me** will live, even though he dies. "*
(John 11:25)

149

*"Yet to all who received him, to **those who believed in his name**, he gave the right to become children of God"*
(John 1:12)
*"Verily, verily, I say unto you,
He that heareth my word, and believeth on him
that sent me, hath everlasting life, and shall not come into
condemnation; but has passed from death to life."*
(John 5:24)
*"For my Father's will is that everyone who looks
to the Son and **believes in him shall have eternal life,**
and I will raise him up at the last day."*
(John 6:40)

**There is NO mention of "sacrament/sacraments"
in the entire Bible, not even once.**
The Lord says:
*"These people come near to me with their mouth
and honor me with their lips, but their hearts
are far from me. Their worship of me is
made up only of rules taught by men."*
(Isaiah 29:13, also in Matthew 15:8, Mark 7:6)

PURGATORY:
Catholics believe
before you can enter Heaven,
you go to a place called "**Purgatory**" (purgatory was
officially declared in 1439 at the Council of Florence
and later reconfirmed at the council of Trent),
**this is a place where one must be punished for a while
until they are purified of their sins.**
Family members can help ancestors exit purgatory faster by
giving more money to the church. Even the Pope himself,
head of the Church (that assumes the existence of
purgatory), must go there to suffer after he dies.

150

Protestant Christians believes
everything the Bible says about Purgatory,
**which is absolutely NOTHING, the word "purgatory"
does not even appear once in the entire Bible.**
Just the mere concept of a "place" that you go to
"suffer your sins" after you die, declares Jesus false,
a liar, and that His perfect sacrifice, was for nothing.
**THE WHOLE IDEA OF "PURGATORY"
COMPLETELY CONTRADICTS JESUS.**

ASSURANCE:
To this day the **Catholic Church** abides that
**"anyone who says they have assurance of salvation
is damned as a Heretic"** (Council of Trent, SessionVI)
this is called **the sin of presumption.**
A "Heretic" is a baptized Roman Catholic who willfully
and persistently rejects **ANY** article of faith.
In fact,
In 1563, at the Council of Trent (session 13, chapter 7),
the Catholic Church made a law, that if anyone was to say
that the bread and wine (used during the Eucharist), was
not the "actual flesh and blood of Christ", would be
punished to death. To think it was "symbolic" as
Protestant Christians believed (and still do),
you were tortured and killed as a Heretic.
It wasn't till years later that the Church
changed its mind, and Protestant
Christians were no longer
"Heretics"
but separated
brethren.

Protestant Christians,
not only believe they are Assured Salvation,
they **PRAISE God** that they have been saved.

151

ASK YOURSELF
is it wise to put your faith **IN MEN,**
even men of church's
or
should you **put your faith in "GODS WORD"?**

God gave us His Word (the Bible) and the
ability to discern against false teachings,
or false prophets, by comparing
them to the Truth found
only in the Bible.

Some of you, may be wondering,
"if all of this is in the Bible,
how could people possibly not see it?"
First of all, many people do (that's why they are "Protestant
Christians"), secondly a lot of people just don't take the
time to read their Bible and discern for themselves.
Jesus said "if the blind lead the blind, will
they not both fall into the ditch".
But many people just figure
if anyone has to know
God and the Bible,
it's the church
Right?

Well if you look in the Bible, you will find
Who constantly attacked Jesus throughout his entire
ministry? Who conspired against him, had him falsely
accused, beaten, and then finally put to death?
It was the "holy leaders" of his time,
the priests who sought to kill
the son of God (unbelievable, but true).
Trust in God, not man.
Trust in God and read His word.

What is Gods Purpose for your life?

_____

_____

_____

_____

_____

_____

_____

_____

_____

_____

_____

My Favorite Bible Verse is...

_____

_____

The Religion of Islam and Christianity
both claim to be the **only** way to God.
Yet their beliefs are so contradictive
that *both* religions can not possibly be right.
Logically speaking, *at least one* of them has to be wrong,
but the question of "which one" has not only confounded
generations in the past, it still divides the world today.

Islam claims the Koran is *the perfect word of God*,
and Christians claim that the Bible is *the word of God*.
So the dilemma remains, which "if either" is correct?
(Please remember that I only say "if either", because I seek
to approach this from a logical perspective, rather than a
faith perspective, and to rely solely upon facts).
But before we can get into *which is right*,
let us ask ourselves some questions:
Why are there so many religions in the world?
Who made up all of these religions?
What has been the primary outcome of so many religions?
Who, if anyone, stands to prosper from so many religions?

Now most of us are familiar with the expression,
that if you want to find out "who did something",
one should first look at "who stood the most to gain",
(today we call this "motive").
So what we really need to ask ourselves is
"Who stands to gain the most from "religions"?
And being that history shows us that *religion*
has been the primary cause of "most wars",
one would then, have to ask themselves,
"Who could possibly desire war"?
Now the only one that comes to my mind is the Liar,
the Deceiver, the Tempter, the prince of this world,
Satan himself, for he is the only one who has the "motive"
and capability to do such, because through the creation of

154

numerous religions, people have become divided
(remember the phrase "divide and conquer"),
and being divided, it is much more difficult for us to
live in peace. Also through the creation of *religions*,
pride has been promoted, for believers usually believe
their religion as "the right one" and everyone else's as
wrong, this seduction of pride, often stimulates feelings
of anger, fear, and/or hatred for the others (who believe
differently), which has ultimately lead us "to war".
Think for a moment,
if the devil really wanted to get back at God (and I mean
really sock it to Him good), what better way for him to do
so, than to create numerous *religions*, so that people (being
God's joyous creation), can go about fighting and killing
each other "all for the love of God". Remember, Satan is
cunning and crafty, he can easily deceive people into
doing evil (such as hating or killing), while causing
them to believe that what they are doing is
nothing more than "God's will".

Therefore, we must constantly guard ourselves against
the enemy, and not give into desires of hate.

Now let us look at two questions
answered first from the Koran
and then from the Bible.

First question
What is one to do, with regards to their Enemies?

The Koran is redundantly specific that anyone who does
not follow the will of Allah is an *infidel* and
"Allah is an enemy to infidels"
(Koran 2:92).

155

"Let not believers take infidels for their friends rather than believers: whoso shall do this has nothing to hope from Allah"
(Koran 3:27).
"Verily the infidels are your undoubted enemies"
(Koran 4:102).
"Fight then against them until strife be at an end, and the religion be all of it Allah's"
(Koran 8:40).
"Make war upon such of those to whom the Scripture have been given as believe not in Allah..."
(Koran 9:29).
"Believers! wage war against such the infidels..."
(Koran 9:123).

Now
with regards to Christianity
the Bible is also redundantly specific, it says,
"Do not resist an evil person, if someone strikes you on the right cheek, turn to him the other also."
(Matthew 5:39).
"But I tell you: Love your enemies and pray for those who persecute you, that you may be sons of your Father in heaven. He causes his sun to rise on the evil and the good, and sends rain on the righteous and the unrighteous. If you love those who love you, what reward will you get? Are not even the tax collectors doing that? And if you greet only your brothers, what are you doing more than others? Do not even pagans do that? Be perfect, therefore, as your heavenly Father is perfect."
(Matthew 5:44-48)
Second question

How is one "Guaranteed" entrance into Heaven?

The Koran says, that one must be slain or die in a *Holy war*
and that this, is the *only way* one can *guarantee* that they
will enter Heaven (Koran 3:151-152, 3:194).
This is why suicide bombers, are so eager to
kill others (and themselves) because it
guarantees them entry into heaven
(according to the Koran).

Now the Bible says,
"Righteousness from God comes through faith in Jesus
Christ to all who believe. There is no difference, for all
have sinned and fall short of the glory of God, and
are justified freely by His grace through the
redemption that came by Christ Jesus."
(Romans 3:22-24)

One says, "to love your enemies," and the other says,
"to kill them". Which is likely a product of deception?

The religion of Islam
is a peaceful religion,
but with regards to non-Muslims,
the Koran declares not to befriend them at all
and if a Muslim is to be attacked they are to respond
in a Jihad (Holy war) where their enemy can either
submit to the will of Allah or be killed.

The religion of Christianity
is a peaceful religion,
but with regards to non-Christians,
the Bible declares to love them and if a Christian is
attacked they are to turn the other cheek and they are
to pray for those who persecute them.

157

Islamic radicals - who follow the Koran to the extreme
do not simply dislike non-Muslims
(a.k.a. infidels), they abhor them with such a passion,
that they dream of having *the honor* of killing as
many of them as they possibly can,
so that they may glorify "Allah".
They also believe so strongly in their faith
that they are more than willing, **to kill for it.**
In this group, people often think of terrorists
such as Osama Bin Laden, and others who
have spread terror on behalf of Islam.

Christian radicals - who follow the Bible to the extreme
do not simply love other Christians, they love everyone,
and seek to share that love through faith in Jesus Christ.
They also believe so strongly in their faith that they are
more than willing, **to die for it**. *Millions have been
slaughtered to death all around the world, simply
for being Christians (even in today's world).*
In this group, people often think of Billy
Graham, Mother Teresa, Dr. Martin
Luther King Jr., and others
who deeply love Jesus.

~

One **NEVER** finds love, on the path of hate.

~

With deception,
the ends always justify the means.

~

One who walks in darkness will be held accountable,
but one who walks in darkness, after seeing the light,
is held accountable *many times over.*

158

"Religions" that contradict themselves:

Many religions state that they "believe in the Bible", but then don't adhere to it's doctrine. Unfortunately this is extremely common. One of the ways they accomplish this is, by referring to the Bible as "incorrect" or "correct but only with the right translation", by doing this "they" (depending on whoever's doing the selling) are then able to state that "they alone" are the "only one's" who know what was is right within scripture.
It is through this <u>perversion</u>, they are then able to completely contradict the Bible.
For example,
If I were to say "I believe in the Bible" and the Bible states within it, that if anyone adds "anything" to it, they are cursed, then I go and say "in addition to the Bible, I believe in 'The Book of Mormon' also" then just by basic common sense, would I not have just cursed myself?

The last chapter of the Bible reads
"For I testify unto every man that heareth the words of the prophecy of <u>this book, If any man shall add unto these things, God shall add unto him the plagues that are written in this book:</u> And if any man shall take away from the words of the book of this prophecy, God shall take away his part out of the book of life, and out of the holy city, and from the things which are written in this book."
(Revelation 22:18)

**After reading that,
would it make any sense,
W H A T S O E V E R
to add anything to the Bible?**

159

The religion of Mormonism:
Also known as
"The Church of Jesus Christ of Latter-day Saints"

Mormons believe that *the God*
who reigns over this world today
was once (long, long ago) a regular man.

A man who had flaws, a man who sinned.
It was only through the religion of Mormonism that the
man **"became a god"** (which he did so on his home planet,
perhaps it was in a galaxy far, far away, or maybe one
nearby). This man became "a God" by dedicating himself
to *The Church of Jesus Christ of Latter-Day Saints* and
after accomplishing all the sanctions and requirements set
forth by the Mormon Church, he was then ordained by **"his
planets God"** to the supreme level of **"Godhood".**
Whereupon becoming a **"new god"**, he was granted a fresh
planet of his very own to rule over (we call that planet
"Earth"). This *former man* then created all the people on
the planet and now reigns over *all of us* as **"God".** God
now seeks to ordain all the "good Mormons" on this planet,
to that same state that he was granted long ago.

Now it is up to each individual to have the insight to follow
the laws and ordinances of **"this world's God"**, and join
the Mormon faith, so that one day **"they to shall become *a
God*"** and be given a planet of their own to rule over.

Mormons believe this cycle continues on and on, so that
The Church of Jesus Christ of Latter-Day Saints can spread
the Mormon faith throughout the entire universe.

And that in a nutshell is what Mormons believe.
Mormons are monotheistic, *with a polytheistic universe.*

160

Mormons also believe that
Jesus and Satan are brothers,
born from *this world's God*, after
having "relations" with Mary.
According to Brigham Young "the second prophet" of
the Mormon Church, *God* had relations with Mary
and being so she gave birth naturally to
a son (Jesus), then later to Satan.
They believe **Jesus was a Polygamist**
married at Cana of Galilee, that Mary, Martha, and others
were his wives, and that he begat children.
(Journal of Discourses, Vol. 2, page 210)

Just incase you missed it the first time,
Mormons believe that <u>YOU</u> can become "a God".
In fact, everyone has the potential to become "a God". At
which point they will receive a temple whereupon, they are
allowed to enter their sacred temples, so that they may go
through a set of secret rituals: baptism for the dead,
celestial marriage, and various oaths of secrecy and
commitment. Also four secret handshakes are taught so that
the believing Mormon, upon entering the third level of
Mormon heaven, can shake hands with a *God* in a certain
pattern, allowing them admittance into the highest level of
heaven.
According to the Book of Mormon (the church's sacred
scripture), God punished Cain for murdering his brother, by
turning the color of his skin dark, and this is the reason why
black people exist and also describes why they claim that
black people are inferior to white people (despite this
doctrine Mormons [since 1978] have been instructed to
believe that black people are no longer inferior).
Yet according to Mormon doctrine:
"If the white man who belongs to the chosen seed,
mixes his blood with the seed of Cain (a black person),

161

the PENALTY, under the LAW OF GOD
IS DEATH ON THE SPOT.
This will ALWAYS BE SO."
(Journal of Discourses, v. 10, p. 110)

It's important to note that although Mormonism was founded with a deep belief in racism, the "Church of Jesus Christ of Latter-Day Saints", presently does it's best to divert attention away from such beliefs (despite all the racist doctrines that still exist within the Mormon Church today). Now one could quite possibly argue, that there have been instances within history whereupon some "Christians" have partook in racism, but one would have to affirm that they did so *only through their own personal accord.* For nowhere in the Bible is racism suggested or promoted as a belief, yet on the contrary Mormon doctrines strongly promote racist beliefs.

"If any man mingle his seed with the seed of Cain the only way he could get rid of it or have salvation would be to come forward and have his head cut off & spill his blood upon the ground it would also take the life of his children..."
(Wilford Woodruff's Journal, recording a speech by Brigham Young, January 16, 1852, typed copy; original located in LDS Church Archives).

Just like racism, Mormons also tend to swerve away from other church doctrines that the Mormon Church was founded upon, such as **"Polygamy"** (whereupon a man can take upon himself numerous wives). Even though Mormons today don't practice polygamy, the founder of Mormonism (Joseph Smith) and other early church leaders depicted "polygamy" as an essential belief to their faith.

Joseph Smith took Helen Mar Kimball as his polygamous

wife at the young age of fourteen (keep in mind he was in
his thirties). Joseph had promised that through her act
of submission to him, she and her parents would be
guaranteed exaltation in the "Celestial Kingdom".
The family believed their daughter's virginity
and submission to Joseph was a small price
to pay, for such a "heavenly" reward.
Being such,
many other families were eager
to offer their daughters for
these kind of "benefits".
Joseph Smith had 30+ wives, many of who were
teenagers and at least eleven of his thirty wives
had legal husbands at the time of their "sealing" to Smith.
Brigham Young had 27 wives and 50+ children.
So one could safely conclude, that polygamy
was a well practiced belief among
it's founder and early leaders.

"The only men who become GODS,
even the Sons of God, are those
WHO ENTER INTO POLYGAMY."
(Journal of Discourses, Vol. 11, page 269)

Mormonism began in 1820,
when young Joseph Smith prayed to know which church he
should join. In answer to his prayer, God the Father and
Jesus Christ appeared to him. They told Joseph that all the
religions of the world were an abomination and false, so
they restored the truth about the plan of God
through Joseph. At the age of twenty-two,
he commenced translation of
"The Book of Mormon"
from golden plates
written in a

163

"reformed Egyptian hieroglyphics"
(a language that has no archeological
support of even existing), into English
by the use of a pair of "magic glasses".
If you desire to read more about the history of Mormonism,
I would suggest reading the book
"One Nation Under God's", *by Richard Abanes.*

It is also important to note that
Mormons strongly consider themselves to be Christian.
Now I'm well aware that anyone could debate over
just about anything, and that being such, if a
Mormon wants to consider them self as
Christian, then who *am I* to say different.
But,
if one concedes that a person "who claims to be Christian",
is not a "True Christian", unless that person believes in
what Jesus taught and abides in that teaching, then one
could only conclude that Mormonism is not a "True
Christian" faith. Due to the fact that Mormon beliefs,
firmly contradict what Jesus taught about God,
salvation, and perhaps most importantly
what Jesus taught about himself.

Since Mormon beliefs constantly
contradict the Bible and deny the deity of Jesus,
many Christians regard
"The Church of Jesus Christ of Latter-Day Saints"
as a distortion of Biblical truth and often refer to them as a
Non-Christian cult.

With that being said,
Christians should always respond to Mormons
in the like manner that they should *any person of any faith*,
with love, respect, and kindness.

The Rich Man and Lazarus

"There was a rich man who was dressed in purple and fine linen and lived in luxury every day. At his gate was laid a beggar named Lazarus, covered with sores and longing to eat what fell from the rich man's table. Even the dogs came and licked his sores.
"The time came when the beggar died and the angels carried him to Abraham's side. The rich man also died and was buried. In hell, where he was in torment, he looked up and saw Abraham far away, with Lazarus by his side. So he called to him, 'Father Abraham, have pity on me and send Lazarus to dip the tip of his finger in water and cool my tongue, because I am in agony in this fire.'
"But Abraham replied, 'Son, remember that in your lifetime you received your good things, while Lazarus received bad things, but now he is comforted here and you are in agony. And besides all this, between us and you a great chasm has been fixed, so that those who want to go from here to you cannot, nor can anyone cross over from there to us.'
"He answered, 'Then I beg you, father, send Lazarus to my father's house, for I have five brothers. Let him warn them, so that they will not also come to this place of torment.'
"Abraham replied, 'They have Moses and the Prophets; let them listen to them.'
" 'No, father Abraham,' he said, 'but if someone from the dead goes to them, they will repent.'
"He said to him, 'If they do not listen to Moses and the Prophets, they will not be convinced even if someone rises from the dead.' "

(Luke 16:19-31)

"No amount of words can ever open a closed heart"
only God can open someone's heart,
but first they must desire for Him to do so.

According to the Bible:
Who is God?
*"...God is love. Whoever lives in
love lives in God, and God in him."*
(1John 4:16)

What is the one true religion?
*"Religion that God our Father accepts as pure and
faultless is this: to look after orphans and widows
in their distress and to keep oneself from
being polluted by the world."*
(James 1:27)

Will everyone who professes Jesus as Lord be saved?
*"Not everyone who says to me, 'Lord, Lord,' will enter
the kingdom of heaven, but only he who does
the will of my Father who is in heaven."*
(Matthew 7:21)

Who is a true believer in Jesus?
*Jesus said, "By this all men will know that you are
my disciples, if you love one another."*
(John 13:35)

Which is greater Faith or Love?
*"And now these three remain: faith, hope and love.
But the greatest of these is love"*
(1Cor 13:13)

The Law of the Prophets,
"...do to others what you would have them do to you..."
(Matthew 7:12))

The Bible in Overview (found in Galatians 3:11)
"...The righteous will live by faith"

IN CLOSING,

I would just like to reiterate, that the descriptions
of the religions found in this book are based solely on
"sacred scripture", writings from "recognized leaders",
and/or "historical facts" pertaining to each particular faith.
Please remember,
that all religions have some level of disagreement's
among believers, and interpretations may vary.
I was strongly tempted to close with my
personal opinions of each religion,
but what I think of them is
irrelevant, the only thing
that matters is, what
you think of
them.

If you are offended by or bare any ill will,
towards any part of my writings,
I apologize and ask that you forgive me.

If you enjoyed this book
or have been touched by any part therein,
I give all praise and glory
to my Lord and Savior
Jesus Christ.
Whether you like me or not, I love you.
God bless

Elijah

Special thanks to my Mom and Dad
for all the love and support they have always given me.

The following pages
are of the utmost importance,
for they are
Your Thoughts on Paper.

By adding your own personal thoughts,
you make this book
precious and absolutely unique.
Therefore,
I have chosen *you*, to finish
"The Wisdom of a Fool"

I was most touched by…

_____

_____

_____

_____

_____

_____

_____

_____

_____

_____

_____

_____

_____

I disagreed with…

_____

_____

_____

_____

_____

_____

_____

_____

_____

_____

_____

_____

_____

_____

Your thoughts on paper…

_____

_____

_____

_____

_____

_____

_____

_____

_____

_____

_____

_____

_____

_____

_____

Your thoughts on paper…

_____

_____

_____

_____

_____

_____

_____

_____

_____

_____

_____

_____

_____

_____

Your thoughts on paper…

_____

_____

_____

_____

_____

_____

_____

_____

_____

_____

_____

_____

_____

_____

Your thoughts on paper…

Your thoughts on paper...

Your thoughts on paper…

_____

_____

_____

_____

_____

_____

_____

_____

_____

_____

_____

_____

_____

_____

Your thoughts on paper…

_____

_____

_____

_____

_____

_____

_____

_____

_____

_____

_____

_____

_____

_____

*"God chose the foolish things of the world
to shame the wise"*
(1COR. 1:27)

May the grace of our Lord Jesus Christ be with you
Today and Always,

Elijah

Printed in the United States
200157BV00003B/169-1524/A